. . . .

"Clever, entertaining, and filled with godly mom-tools. This book is just what a crazy-stressed mom needs. And I'm rather an expert in *crazy*. I knew it up close and personal even before I had five babies. *In seven years.* We're talking layered crazy. That's one reason I so love, and so get, *Too Blessed to be Stressed for Moms.* Debora Coty offers some sweet chuckles between the pages of this book. Some poignant moments too. But it's more than either of those things. Along with the smiles and a gasp of surprise or a tear-dab, we find practical, biblical how-tos to help us deal successfully with the *crazy* of motherhood—all by and through the power of Christ."

—Rhonda Rhea, TV personality, humor columnist, and author or coauthor
of twelve books, including *Turtles in the Road* and *Fix-Her-Upper*

"Debora Coty's done it again—she's hijacked the humor in motherhood. And through the laughter, Debora weaves support, reassurance, and encouragement for every beleaguered mom, while morphing the funny to functional with tips and questions designed to help moms unpack the beat-myself-up baggage we've all carried at one time or another. Don't miss this book!"

—Deb DeArmond, speaker and award-winning author of
marriage and family books, including *I Choose You Today*
and *Don't Go to Bed Angry: Stay Up and Fight!*

"I'm always smiling while reading Debora Coty's books. In *Too Blessed to be Stressed for Moms,* Deb uses her delightful gift of storytelling to deliver another round of well-timed truth that nourishes us right where we are, while gently nudging us ever closer to our good, good Father."

—Shellie Rushing Tomlinson, speaker and author of
Devotions for the Hungry Heart

"The most difficult title I've ever held was that of Mom. While raising my kids, every day seemed filled with reasons to doubt decisions, question my sanity, and call on God for help. *Too Blessed to be Stressed for Moms* is a must-read for every mom. You will find yourself laughing at Debora's humor and wittiness while you digest her solid and helpful biblical guidance. Her understanding perspective will leave you feeling like you're sitting down with your best friend who 'gets it' and is in your mom corner. If you're a mom, you will love this book!"

—Lucille Williams, author of *From Me to We*

"Hey, moms, if you're struggling to keep your head above water, Debora Coty knows what your life is like. She's changed diapers, smashed peas, cleaned cat vomit, and lived to tell the tale! This book is the perfect way to unwind after a crazy-full day of parenting and get refreshed and recharged for the next one. You can do this, Mom! Debora can help."

—Margot Starbuck, speaker and award-winning author

"Debora Coty's newest book feels like peeking into a diary of someone you admire, reading oh-so-vulnerable moments that make you sigh in relief. Deb comes alongside moms with delicious humor, gently steering them to rely on God's promises to make something wonderful out of something frizzled and frazzled."

—Suzanne Woods Fisher, bestselling author of dozens of Amish fiction and nonfiction books, including *Amish Peace: Simple Wisdom for a Complicated World*

"Debora knows how it goes. Her sense of humor and voice of truth give moms the choice to laugh at the moments we might otherwise cry over. This book is a pocket of delight."

—Tricia Lott Williford, author of *You Can Do This*

"Wow! Finally, a book that gets a mama's heart. You'll love this encouragement through the crazy-busy—and the sometimes crazy-messy—moments of momhood. *Too Blessed to be Stressed for Moms* is a hilarious and insightful reminder that God is standing by to bless it all. So grab a glass of iced tea, this book, and Debora's cue for a mommy time-out. You'll be blessed through the very last page."

—Beth Duewel, writer, speaker, blogger, and coauthor of *Fix-Her-Upper: Hope and Laughter through a God Renovated Life*

"Deb Coty offers up a refreshing dose of humor with her wisdom gleaned from decades of motherhood. Reading this book felt like a mentor encouraging me to lighten up and keep perspective on the big picture of parenting with God's grace front and center!"

—Courtney Westlake, author of *A Different Beautiful*

"*Too Blessed to be Stressed* is my kind of book. . .simple, funny, and straight to the point. I'm a mom; I don't have time to read anything except something that's going to help me *and* also make me laugh. If you're a mom needing either of those things, this book is for you! Grab a doughnut and settle in for a good read!"

—Kerri Pomarolli, author of *Moms' Night Out and Other Things I Miss*, comedian, and actress appearing on *The Tonight Show*, Comedy Central, and ABC

"Read this book. Discover the mysteries of BOOP and Hot Fudge Verses. See mothering anew as you gaze at the Good Samaritan. Thank God that Debora lets you peer into her human Mom Moments that we all have but would rather hide. And most of all? Hug tightly this message: It's never too late to be your best Mom-self."

—Dr. Naomi Cramer Overton, past president and CEO of MOPS (Mothers of Preschoolers) International and advocate for children with World Vision and Compassion International

"Moms need boatloads of encouragement. And empathy. Humor. Practical help. And they need it delivered in a way that is fun and easy to read between rocking babies, taming tantrums, or easing a kid's latest heartache. Deb Coty is a delightful writer, and I always come away from her stories and tidbits of down-home wisdom feeling hugged and lifted up. I guarantee that you will too!"

—Becky Johnson, coauthor of *Nourished: A Search for Health, Happiness and a Full Night's Sleep* and *We Laugh, We Cry, We Cook* www.laughcrycook.com

"Deb Coty offers wise, seasoned perspective and encouragement in her devotional, *Too Blessed to be Stressed for Moms*. Her witty insight is exactly what us mamas need in our chaotic season: truth, humor, and practical reminders that God is real and present in every detail of our day. I especially love her hot fudge verses. Because, well. . .*hot fudge*."

—Bekah Pogue, author of *Choosing REAL*, speaker, soul carer, and writer at bekahpogue.com

Too Blessed to be Stressed for Moms

Debora M. Coty

SHILOH RUN  PRESS

An Imprint of Barbour Publishing, Inc.

Member of the
Evangelical Christian
Publishers Association

Printed in China.

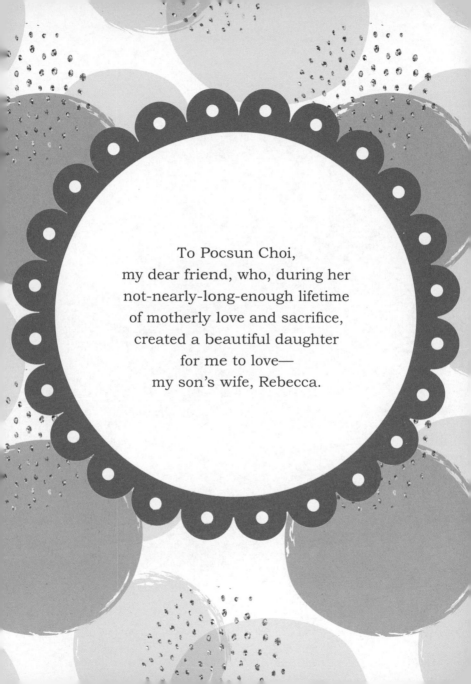

To Pocsun Choi,
my dear friend, who, during her
not-nearly-long-enough lifetime
of motherly love and sacrifice,
created a beautiful daughter
for me to love—
my son's wife, Rebecca.

Contents

• •

Introduction 11

Stress Test for Moms 12

SECTION 1: Why Didn't Anybody Warn Me?

1. PMS: Pretending Mom's Sane (Motherhood Mayhem) ... 16

2. I'm Not Crazy—I'm Crazy-Busy (Seeking Balance) 23

3. Unbuttoning My Attitude (Finding Room to Breathe).... 29

4. Moms Wearing Training Pants (Parenting Styles) 36

5. Prison Break (Scaling My Fences) 45

6. I'll Pencil You In at 4:53 (Time Management) 55

SECTION 2: So Where's the Ding-Dang Motherhood Manual?

7. Lipstick on a Pig (Hidden Wounds)............................... 64

8. Thinking Outside the (Sand)Box (Being Enough).......... 72

9. Becoming You-Nique (Finding My Mothering Niche) 80

10. Blabber Control Issues (Sometimes Ya Just Gotta Laugh) 87

11. Too Blessed to be Obsessed (Letting Go of Mom-Guilt).. 95

12. Chocolate Caulks Relationship Cracks (Forgiveness)......103

SECTION 3: Coloring My World with the Crayons Papa God Gives Me

13. Detoxifying My Stinky Face (Encouraging Others)...... 112

14. Zombie in Sweats (Finding Elusive Rest).................... 121

15. Mommas in the Trenches (Mom-Courage)................. 128

16. My Hair Stylist Is from Oz (Confidence)...................... 137

17. Ripening Isn't Just for Bananas (Everyday Miracles)......145

18. Gratitude Is Glade for the Soul (Developing a
    Thankful Lifestyle)... 152

SECTION 4: Mothering Is a Lifetime Gig

19. They're Not Crow's-Feet; They're Chuckle Crinkles
    (Choose Laughter) 162

20. Letting Yourself Go (Emotional Damage Control)........ 169

21. Call Me Thrill Rider (Finding Adventure
    in the Mundane).. 177

22. Morphing This Worrier into a Warrior (Worry)............. 184

23. Patience Should Be a Verb (Perseverance).................. 193

24. Give Yourself Some Grace (Hangin' Tough)................. 202

25. So How Does This Mom-Gig End? (Living in Hope)..... 210

Introduction

. . . .

*F*eeling like you're totally Mom-Mom-Mom-Mom'ed out? Or so stressed, you're a ticking mom-bomb? As in. . ."Take cover, she's gonna blow!"

I *so* get that. It's only because you're an overworked, overtapped, over-sucked-out mother who's barely treading water in the stress-pool of life.

We moms constantly deal with unexpected disruptions, overflows, explosions, implosions, boo-boos, bodily fluids not our own, emergencies that aren't, emergencies that are, and uncharted potholes that career us off our preferred path. It's all part of the job description.

To add insult to misery, the countless things we do for our families often go unnoticed and unappreciated. *Sigh.* What a comfort to know that the Creator of all things sees everything, no matter how small.

Our reward may not be Mother of the Year. It may not be hugs and kisses. It may not be here on earth at all. (I'm hoping it'll be a maid and cook for all eternity.) Whatever it is, we'll be thrilled because our loving heavenly Parent is pleased with us. "Your Father, who sees what is done in secret, will reward you" (Matthew 6:4 NIV).

Dearest sister-mom, if you're a stress mess, this one's for you.

My books aren't written for the have-it-all-together, but for the scattered and tattered, scarred and scared. We'll tackle topics like mom-guilt, worry, time management, emotional damage control, finding room to breathe, and simply being *enough*.

I pray that my crazy mom stories, encouragement from Papa God ("Abba" in biblical Aramaic), and a whole heap of LOLs within these pages will bring you hope, even if it's the size of a brownie crumb.

It'll be enough for you to take the next bold plunge toward honest-to-goodness joy.

• •

Stress Test for Moms

*W*hether you're reading this book individually or with girlfriends (the discussion questions at the end of each chapter make it perfect for small group Bible studies), this little stress test will help you discover your stress level starting point.

☐ T ☐ F The voice in my head is usually screaming.

☐ T ☐ F The running of my household primarily falls to me.

☐ T ☐ F During an average twenty-four-hour day, I sleep less than six hours.

☐ T ☐ F I can't remember the last time I saw my car floorboards.

☐ T ☐ F The drive-through guy at our fave fast-food place knows me by name.

☐ T ☐ F My idea of a good time is a whole hour by myself.

☐ T ☐ F I am better described by the word *frazzled* than *dazzled*.

☐ T ☐ F After 9:00 p.m., I am usually too exhausted to even think about romance.

☐ T ☐ F My forgot-to-do list is almost as long as my to-do list.

☐ T ☐ F If worry were an Olympic event, I'd be a gold medalist.

Now count the answers you marked "true" and check out your status:

1–4: Yellow Alert! You are at risk of becoming stressed out.

5–7: Orange Alert! Look out—you're at toxic stress levels.

8–10: Red Alert! The siren is blaring and you need immediate stress intervention!

Section 1

. . . .

Why Didn't Anybody Warn Me?

❧◦❧

The quickest way for a mother to get her kids'
attention is to sit down and look comfortable.
—NEW OLD SAYING

If you wait for perfect conditions,
you will never get anything done.
ECCLESIASTES 11:4 TLB

CHAPTER 1

PMS: Pretending Mom's Sane

· ·

Motherhood Mayhem

If I keep my eyes on God,
I won't trip over my own feet.
PSALM 25:15 MSG

❧

*A*s a first-time, expectant mom, I smiled in breathless awe as I prepared the baby's room, washing crinkly stiffness out of brand-new crib sheets, smoothing them to perfection over the mattress of the newly assembled crib, and arranging— then rearranging—adorable baby animal–themed mobiles and pillows in anticipation of the arrival of my precious son.

Every morning I stood by my baby's bed and lovingly patted the sacred, hallowed place he would lay his sweet little head.

Then one day, my hand came up hairy. What was this? Cat hair? In my baby's bed? *No. No. NO!*

I hid behind the couch, spying on our snowy-white cat,

Shawna. Sure enough, she'd taken to jumping up and sleeping in the crib. In the all-about-me nature of felines, she'd apparently assumed that her humans had provided this soft new domicile just for her napping pleasure. After all, up to that point, she'd been the sole recipient of our love and attention—our furry baby.

Okay. Surely this misunderstanding could be resolved. Shawna simply had to learn her boundaries.

I gently shooed her out. She leaped right back in.

I hoisted her out of the forbidden crib and transplanted her to the opposite side of the house. Ten minutes later, she was back, whiskers bristling and tail twitching in annoyance.

"Nuh-uh, you bad girl!" I fussed, attempting to use her food bowl as redirection. She turned up her nose and hightailed it back to the nursery.

I chased her with a shoe. She hissed at me.

Do demons possess cats?

The war was on. But that strong-willed feline kept winning every battle.

So I shut the door. Shawna would surely forget about the crib during the remaining weeks until the baby came.

Ahhh. Enter beautiful baby Matthew. His name means "God's gift."

Yep, that's what we tell people, anyway.

In truth (now don't judge me, girlfriend), Chuck and immensely pregnant I chose that name during a midnight showing of *Invasion of the Body Snatchers* at the local theater. The lead character Matthew (played by Donald Sutherland) was being chased by human-replacing aliens hatched from grotesquely throbbing, mucus-oozing, casket-sized pea pods (inspiring plot, right?). After we'd listened to evil aliens shout, "Mat-thewww. . . Mat-thewww. . . ," for two hours, the name sorta stuck.

But hey, it sounds a lot Christian-er to say he's "God's gift," don't you think?

I digress.

So we brought our delightful bundle of joy home from the hospital, took a bazillion photos, beamed as relatives, friends, and neighbors oohed and aahed, then tiptoed into the nursery to lay the sleeping infant in his crib.

But someone was already there.

Shawna had reclaimed her territory.

The battle of wills resumed, both sides more ardent than ever: In, out. In, out. In, OUT!

Then the dreadful last straw when I peeked in to check on my peacefully sleeping baby and found the infernal cat draped across his warm little head.

"That's it!" I cried. "You're outta here!" Snatching Shawna up like a four-legged rag doll, I heaved her out the front door. "See how you like being an outdoor cat from now on."

Well, she didn't like it one smidgen, no ma'am. That stubborn critter dashed inside every time the door opened, only to be rounded up and tossed back out. Her outrage was palpable. Hell hath no fury like a female scorned. . .regardless of the species. She was one torqued, snarling, revengeful soul, let me tell you.

Then one Sunday morning I found her perched on the couch like the queen she was convinced she was. She'd apparently snuck in and decided to demonstrate her smug sovereignty.

Ousted yet again. But wait. Something seemed. . .off.

On the ride to church, I kept sniffing. Hmm. Did the baby need a diaper change? No, but something wasn't right; I just couldn't put my finger on it.

A faint acrid odor kept niggling my senses during the worship songs. Then as the pastor began preaching, I reached into my purse for a pen to take notes. *Yikes! What in the world?* It was sopping wet in there! I held up my dripping pen and a sodden roll of Life Savers—now black and slimy—as the sharp *ewww* of ammonia slapped heads in my direction.

Cat urine. That spiteful cat had taken revenge by peeing in my purse.

How she managed to straddle my open purse (a male I could understand, but a female?) will forever remain a mystery, but everything in there was completely ruined. My wallet and all it contained. . .saturated. And the horrific smell! *Gag.* I ended up having to throw that purse and its contents away. Except the cash. I'm far too, um, frugal (some might even say tightwadical) for that.

The only positive consequence was that it was a great excuse to spend those reeking bills faster than a bride at Bloomingdale's. I deftly ignored the wrinkled noses and arched eyebrows of the poor cashiers handling the nasty stuff. They doubtless thought I'd fished it out of a sewer.

Sigh. Just another day in a mother's life, right?

Challenges are definitely part of the motherhood download. No getting around it, so we just have to get through it. Not only must we manage the moods and ravages of our own roller-coaster hormones, we somehow have to juggle the craziness balls of everyone else under our roof.

Jealous pets are just one of the milder hazards. Between midnight colic, leaky diapers, projectile vomiting, weapons of mass destruction (toddlers), car-seat chaos, skinned appendages, gum-matted hair, sibling crash dummies, trampled feelings, adolescent hormonal tsunamis, and endless teen angst, moms must grope deep inside their battered souls for compassion. And a few slivers of humor wouldn't hurt.

Thankfully, our Creator thought of everything. Did you know pregnancy actually alters a woman's brain, changing the size and structure of areas involved in emotional attachment to their young? A recent *Nature Neuroscience* study found that motherly nurturing skills—like perceiving the feelings and perspectives of others—are enhanced in pregnancy and continue for at least two years after giving birth.[1] Darn good thing too.

Wouldn't it be awesome if this extra helping of grace and forbearance lasted throughout those turbulent teen years? But hey, we'll be grateful for any crumbs we get and do the best we can.

Even if it sometimes feels like it's not enough.

Like when we make awful parenting mistakes. When we drop those do-it-all juggling balls. When we're positive our kids will turn out to be serial killers.

I'll never forget the day my teenage daughter informed me that she'd probably be in therapy for years due to my mothering. *Ouch.*

My response? "Well, it's your job to be a better mother than you had. It was my job and my mother's and her mother's before that. Keep all the good stuff and improve on the bad. One day in the future, maybe one of our descendants will get it right."

Listen, sister-mom, we don't have to wallow in shame over our mothering mistakes. Every single one of us makes 'em. Some hide them better than others, but we *all* fail at times. And it's okay. Really, it is. Papa God created us as imperfect, stumbling, what-was-I-thinking humans, knowing we'd be raising offspring just as flawed as we are.

The good news is that our heavenly Father loves us to pieces anyway. And wants us to look to Him as the *only* example of a perfect parent.

So guess what? Ten years after my daughter's doomful pronouncement of my mothering deficiencies, she and her husband bought the house next door to us. Go figure. They now *intentionally* include me in every aspect of raising their three children. I rejoice that my maternal mistakes have somehow been smoothed over. Redemption is sweet!

And despite your misgivings, sweet thang, your redemption will be too. No matter how badly you think you're screwing up today. It's called God's grace.

So please don't beat yourself up with the vicious lie that you're the worst mother in the history of the world. You're not. Nor was I, although I would've bet the farm on it many days. You cannot judge your worth by your current circumstances. Don't allow yourself to fall into the emotional black hole of self-condemnation; Papa God's love for you is immeasurably bigger than your biggest blunders.

Well, except for the time you barbecued your cat. Oh. Wait. That was me.

Just kidding, cat lovers—Shawna wouldn't fit on the grill (I measured). She finally adapted to her outdoor abode and happily straddled flower pots to a ripe old age. How proud I am that she learned that skill on my purse.

• •

Sign on church marquee:
COME ON INSIDE.
WE'RE ALL MESSED UP.
YOU'LL FIT RIGHT IN.

• •

Navigating the 'Hood (the MotherHood)

1. What were some of your biggest challenges as a new mother? How did you make it through?

2. Which do-it-all balls you're currently juggling are the hardest to keep in the air?

3. Do you struggle with self-condemnation? It's okay to admit it. . .every mom does from time to time. How about pausing right now to lift those nagging feelings of failure up to your heavenly Father? You just never know what kind of redemption He has in store for you.

4. What keeps you sane in the midst of the motherhood mayhem? Hey, girlfriend, when you feel like life's falling apart, I know a really BIG Someone with a really BIG glue gun.

CHAPTER 2

I'm Not Crazy—I'm Crazy-Busy

· ·

Seeking Balance

I will strengthen you, surely I will help you.
ISAIAH 41:10 NASB

～୬ଡ଼ଚ～

*H*ey, did you hear about twenty-seven-year-old Amber Miller, who, in her thirty-eighth week of pregnancy, completed the 26.2-mile Chicago Marathon then checked into a hospital to plunk out a healthy baby girl?

Now that's what I call a mom on the fly!

Well, you and I might not officially run marathons, but we both know our feet fly at a marathoner's pace most days. So many things we *must* do; a few things we *want* to do; and countless things we *should* do.

You know, *should* is a dangerous word. It's a stress-filled, pressure-packed slave driver. It ruthlessly inflates the bulk of a mother's to-do list, often crowding out healthy sanity-essentials with guilt-induced clutter.

* "I *should* go to that parents' meeting; in a weak moment, I said I'd be treasurer."

* "My mother thinks I *should* cook a big dinner every night like she did."

* "I really *should* make time to bake a pie for my new neighbor."

* "*Shouldn't* I crochet cute beanies for my kids like Perfect Patti does?"

* "I *should* clean my house so the kids won't write notes in the dust."

Our *shoulds* may be fueled by self-comparisons with friends and neighbors, subtle cultural messages, high expectations imposed on us by church, civic, or family members, or maybe even unrealistic regulations we've self-inflicted to become a perfect mother. . .as if that fairy-tale creature really exists.

But as every woman striving to squeeze into last year's skinny jeans knows, more isn't always better; sometimes it's simply overwhelming. You know, we can be whelmed without being overwhelmed. *Whelmed* is livable; *overwhelmed* is strangling. We just have to recognize that we truly do have the power to choose which *shoulds* are potential *coulds*. . .and then unapologetically embrace the woman our choices make us.

Only then can we clear the choking clutter and take a deep, cleansing, reinvigorating breath. *Whew.* The pressure is now manageable.

Once when I was playing baseball with my preschool grandbuddy, Blaine, his mama started filming. Suddenly I couldn't pitch the ball straight for love nor money. "Whoa! The pressure's on!" I acknowledged, throwing the ball everywhere but over the plate.

Blaine, wise beyond his five years, calmly laid down his bat, reached for an imaginary faucet valve, turned it, and said, "Okay, Mimi. Now the pressure's off. Play ball!"

Yep, sometimes we need to take the initiative to turn off the pressure valve and just play ball. Here are a few tried-and-true suggestions to stymie the flow:

* *Be stress-smart.* When you're slammed into a stress mess, sit yourself down and have a calming cup of your fave hot beverage and a snack (*not* baby carrots—something satisfying but not too fattening so you don't add calorie remorse to your stress baggage). Close your eyes. Tune in to Papa God's loving presence. . .His heartbeat. . .His peace. Slap guilt to the curb when the tyranny of the urgent attacks; *you* are important. Everything else can wait a few minutes. I promise you the world will not end while you regroup. Unless the kids start a fire in your panty drawer.

* *Move to the front.* Promote yourself off the back burner. Don't argue, girl, just do it. You may sacrificially place yourself there routinely, but your Creator doesn't. You're a front-burner person to Him. He wants you to enjoy this marvelous gift of life He's given you, not sludge through it. So it's time to add a little fun to your day. Write yourself into your schedule for an hour of

something you enjoy a minimum of three days a week—walk in the sunshine, bike a woodsy trail, sing, boogie, dig in your garden until you find Papa God there, get your nails done—whatever tingles your toes. Put that beautiful smile back on your face. And speaking of pots on burners. . .

✳ *Avoid BOOP—Boiling Oatmeal Overflow Phenomenon.* BOOP is one of my Coty Near-Facts of Science (theories not yet proven by actual scientific studies but nonetheless known by women to be true). You see, I postulate that women are like pots of oatmeal; at the beginning of the day we simmer—little manageable bubbles of stress rise to the surface and harmlessly pop. But as the day progresses, the heat escalates and the oatmeal boils higher and wilder and meaner until it overflows and spoils everything around with a nasty, ugly, sticky mess. The key to avoiding BOOP is to know when to remove the pot from the heat.

✳ *Be a dipstick.* The Lord puts only enough fuel in your daily tank for you to arrive safely at the destination He's routed out for you. All the detours you add will either run you out of gas or land you in a ditch. Check your tank, review your destination, and then engage in the Three Ps: Prioritize, Plan, and Pace yourself.

Listen, you don't have to end up like the disheveled, disillusioned woman standing beside me at a high school graduation party who muttered with a weary sigh, "My children suck the marrow out of my bones."

Nope, you can be like my friend Debbie, mother of nine (yes,

I said *nine*), who pronounced in the middle of her mothering marathon, "Resting and waiting can be more faith-filling than doing and overachieving."

She's right. It's all about keeping your balance as you pound the pavement.

• •

> *My mother is my travel agent*
> *for a lifelong guilt trip.*
> —Seen on a bumper sticker

• •

Navigating the 'Hood

1. What are some of the *shoulds* that clutter your to-do list? Name two *should* items you can prune from your current list to begin decluttering.

2. Do you tend to put yourself on the back burner? In which ways? Do you think this pleases Papa God, who lovingly created you and loves to see you—His precious daughter—smile? (I begin to grasp my true worth when I consider that my heavenly Father feels the same way about me that I feel about my own beloved children. . .on a good day!)

3. Does my BOOP theory apply to your average day? How?

4. So, dear one, will you intentionally remove your pot from the burner? Let's review the Three Ps:

　＊　Prioritize

　＊　Plan

　＊　Pace yourself

How can you practice these Ps in your current circumstances?

CHAPTER 3

Unbuttoning My Attitude

· ·

Finding Room to Breathe

It is for freedom that Christ has set us free.
GALATIANS 5:1 NIV

*W*hat kind of volcano-erupting pressure drives people nuts like the Orlando mother who chased the bully of her nine-year-old daughter, threw the kid off his bicycle, and slammed him into a concrete wall? After choking him and threatening death, she drove him home.

The woman later told police she didn't intend to hurt the boy.[1]

Um. . .*what?*

Well, maybe you and I don't intend to hurt anyone either, but when unrelenting stress takes its toll and that molten lava of passion begins surging from our innards, we lose control. It erupts in rage and frustration and people get burned— sometimes people we love.

I'm guessing one of the reasons this woman popped her cork was because she was an overworked, overtapped, over-sucked-out mom. Like me. Like you.

Sister-mom, are you stressed under? Does everything feel like it's heaped on top of you and you're unable to wriggle out from beneath the pile?

If so, you need an intervention before your hope gets smothered under there. Not to scare you, but hopelessness is a very real possibility. Its seeds are planted amid relentless busyness, and you don't realize it's taken root and started to kudzu your spirit until you can no longer envision a tomorrow that isn't as bleak as today. (If you're north of the Mason-Dixon, you might need to Google "kudzu vine," the green plague that's smothering the South.)

With our attention splintered a dozen ways at once, the symptoms of being overly stressed can blindside us: unexplained upset stomach, headaches, muscle or joint pain, irritability, inability to focus, insomnia, sudden outbursts of anger, binge eating or loss of appetite, chronic fatigue, sullenness, lack of interest in things you used to enjoy.

Any of these chirp your ringtone?

Okay then. It's time to take care of your own needs for a while. Your body is telling you (gut problems), your spirit is telling you (yes, it absolutely *is* spiritual warfare!), and your emotions are telling you (anxiety): *Help! I need a change!*

When the jeans on your attitude are inflicting a wedgie, you need to unbutton. Adjust. Loosen your uptight. Anxiety is Satan's best tool to burn us out and make us flimsy, one-dimensional Flat Stanleys when we could be Robust Robertas.

When the devil's got that anxiety noose around your neck and he's rocking the stool, try some of these angst-melting tips:

* *Jive with the beat.* Neuroscience studies have found that when people listen to their favorite music, they often experience a high similar to that caused by eating chocolate or having sex. *Whoa.* Dopamine, a pleasure-inducing chemical, is released in the brain, producing an emotional rush, with reactions spanning from relaxed smiles to curled toes. Yes, please. Uplift your attitude. Get your bad self down. Blame that tune.

* *Become your own manager.* Cliché, maybe, but still smart: just say no. People—even well-meaning, God-fearing, good-hearted people—will drain your time and energies because they're clueless about the stress you're under and simply see you as fresh meat to help promote their causes. Good causes, sure. Maybe even righteous causes. But hear me now: unless you draw the line, the pressure will *never* let up. It's human nature to try to wring every drop of blood out of the turnip (that's you). It's up to you to manage the limited energy Papa God has allotted you. . .who else will? Discern what's worth your precious time. Become a choice-making manager rather than a spirit-sagging custodian, picking up the chewed-up, spit-out pieces of you.

* *Choose your focus.* Actually, choose three. Only three areas of ministry (such as family, job, BFF time, Bible study group, your personal mission, meeting the new neighbors, etc.) to focus on this week. Pray about which. Decide. Write them down. Say no to everything else.

That's n-o. Next week, repeat the process. Stick to your focus priorities. Your stress will be drastically reduced and you might even find a little extra breathing space. Hey, sometimes we simply must unclog our constipated calendar with an activity enema. Helpful hint: When you're praying about priorities, the wrong question to ask is, "Are You with me on this, Lord?" Instead, ask, "Am I with *You* on this, Lord?" Listen for His answers; they come in unexpected and diverse ways. It's often in life's incidental moments that Jehovah speaks the loudest.

✳ *Protect your mind.* Okay, prepare yourself—this one's radical: limit your news exposure to once per day. Now I'm not saying play ostrich and bury your ignorant head in the sand; I'm encouraging you to live Philippians 4:8 (MSG) out loud: "You'll do best by filling your minds and meditating on things true, noble, reputable, authentic, compelling, gracious—the best, not the worst; the beautiful, not the ugly; things to praise, not things to curse." Of course you should be aware of current world events, but that doesn't mean you must wallow in them. We all know media news is 90 percent negative—death, destruction, evil. Horror makes good headlines. So pick your poison (media outlet) and limit its depressing input to once daily. Try it. You'll be surprised what an anxiety-relieving difference it'll make in your general her-spective. You might even find yourself humming as you pluck your unibrow.

✳ *Take a mom's time-out.* Regardless of the ages of your kids, it's very, very important to periodically take a few minutes to revive and regroup. Your longevity depends on it. Bask in the sunshine, call a girlfriend, finish that fabulous Deb Coty book, or even hide in your closet. Seriously. That's what I did when my kiddos were young. Set a ten-minute timer outside the closet door, and when those little fingers come creeping underneath, state firmly: "Hello. You have reached Mom's time-out. Please leave your name and number and I'll return your call when the timer dings." (Oh, and be sure to keep a stash of non-crinkly-wrapped *quiet* chocolate on your top shelf for these little personal time-outs.)

* *Unplug.* If you've read my other books (and I do hope you have), you already know how crucial I believe this is. Schedule a He-and-Me Retreat: three hours, once a month, just you, your Creator, and your Bible and journal, somewhere quiet and secluded (preferably a nearby park, lake, woodsy area, even your own backyard when no one is home). I know—it sounds impossible. But it really isn't if you view refilling your empty spiritual tank as important as it truly is. And believe me, you're at risk of being shattered into teensy anxiety shards if you don't make time for spiritual restoration. Farm the kids out, turn off all electronics (yes, even your phone!), and spend the first hour simply resting (maybe chin-deep in a hot bubble bath?). Chill, baby. The second hour is spent reading your Bible and praying. The third hour is for prayer walking somewhere inspiring—in the woods, near a lake, through a nice neighborhood. Walk with no agenda; just listen for Papa God's still, small voice speaking to your heart and thank Him for everything that comes to mind. Daydream with Him

about what you'd like to do or where you'd like to go, or what you'd like to see one day. Something that makes you grin. Now take it a step further. . .

✳   *Make fun.* Do something fun at least once a week. Schedule it and look forward to it all week. It can be with the fam or not, but the point is it must be as stress-free as possible and something that *you* enjoy. Key word here: en*joy*. You need to recover your joy. Joy is one of the first casualties of stress; rescuing joy rescues *you*.

So, girlfriend, next time you feel the molten anxiety lava beginning to boil in your innards and fight a mombo urge to chase down a sassy kid on a bike, unbutton your attitude before it bursts at the seams. Or gets you tossed in the slammer.

• •

If evolution is true, how come
mothers only have two hands?
—MILTON BERLE

• •

Navigating the 'Hood

1.   Describe a time when your inner volcano erupted and you felt out of control. Was anyone burned by the gush of lava?

2.   Can you pinpoint any stress symptoms that have crept into your life recently?

3. Do you ever feel that hopelessness is moving in and overtaking your spirit like kudzu? Name one thing you can do each week to keep hope alive and healthy.

4. What are some ways you can apply the angst-melting tips listed in this chapter to reduce your own inner-volcano pressure?

CHAPTER 4

Moms Wearing Training Pants

. . . .

Parenting Styles

*Train a child in the way he should go,
and when he is old he will not turn from it.*
PROVERBS 22:6 NIV

Thud. Thud. Screech! I stood outside my almost-three-year-old daughter's room, gripping the doorknob, tears dripping down my face.

There it was again: *Thud. Thud. Screech!* It felt like my heart ramming into my rib cage. But no. It was my strong-willed child slamming her head against the closed door then screaming in pain.

This was supposed to be her time-out, her punishment for willfully disobeying. She was supposed to be sitting in the tiny red chair, isolated for five minutes in her room, reflecting on the consequences of naughtiness. She was supposed to be concluding that it was a better idea to obey Mommy than to run with forbidden scissors and hack off a hunk of her own hair.

But she wasn't.

Thud. Thud. Screech! Her little blond head indented the wood as she vented her outrage. I felt like a complete mom-failure. This whole mess had played out like a nightmare.

After the sixth time Mommy chased her through the house to repark her diapered derriere in the time-out chair, Mommy, by now immersed in her own irate snit, resorted to manually holding the doorknob. If the little urchin wouldn't stay in the chair, at least she'd stay in the room. But when her escape route was blocked, the wee darlin' began using her head as a wrecking ball.

Sigh. What's a mom to do? It's no wonder mother guppies devour their young.

According to scripture, discipline is directly related to our peace of mind as mothers: "Discipline your children, and they will give you happiness and peace of mind" (Proverbs 29:17 NLT). Right. It just doesn't say how long or hard or what kind of discipline to use until that elusive peace shows up.

The challenge is in finding what type of discipline works for each child, whose personality, intelligence, and level of sensitivity dictate how they individually respond. Even children in the same family don't respond the same.

The scenario above never would've happened with my son. Firstborn, compliant, and eager to please, Matthew generally responded immediately and favorably to "No!" or the look. You know. The one that can melt a Plymouth. That, combined with the time-out chair and an occasional glimpse at the ominous wooden spoon, was all he needed to mend his errant ways. (Reckon conformity has anything to do with a cat sleeping across your face in infancy?)

Not my daughter, no, nope, no ma'am. Disciplining Cricket was like taming a baby tiger—she was hardheaded, fearless, and defiant, eager to explore the world on her own terms and rarely deterred by punishment. By the way, if you have one of these, take heart; their younger selves are nothing like the adults they'll become. Cricket grew into a smart, loving, sensitive woman—now my best friend—with a couple of baby tigers of her own to tame [wicked snicker].

In fact—a little side story here—Cricket was so timid in high school (the exact opposite of her elementary self) that when I called her during the prom and asked how it was going, she replied, "I've been sitting at a table the whole time, Mom. It's going that way." So I did what any sincerely concerned, excellent-advice-offering mama would do. I belted out Lee Ann Womack's "I Hope You Dance" over the phone. And honey, I totally infused all the soulful passion I could muster into the last line: "And when you get the choice to sit it out or dance, I hope you'll dance!"

The thing I didn't know was that Cricket had put me on speaker and moved me to the center of the table. I was entertaining a dozen amused, overdressed, cynical teenagers. I caught on when they burst into hoots and applause at the end. At least my kid's friends have good musical taste.

Well, awkward impromptu concerts may not be your parenting groove. And that's cool. We all experience different styles of parenting and discipline (or lack thereof) while growing up, and we've chosen to raise our children by either mirroring our own parents' child-raising techniques or scrambling to do the exact opposite (more about this in chapter 9).

Behavior scientists have identified four basic parenting styles, although there are numerous variations and combinations of characteristics related to our personalities. I find it easier to think of these styles in terms of animals, so the animal analogies are mine. Do you recognize yourself in any of these?

1. Polar Bears (psychologists call this style "Authoritative")

Daddy Polar Bear is outta there after a one-night stand, while knocked-up Mama Bear puts on an average of four hundred pounds during her pregnancy (just like me!). Newborns are blind and toothless—totally helpless. They stay by Mama Bear's side for two years before lumbering off on their own, during which time the cubs are swaddled in bear hugs (where did you think that term came from?) and nurtured with attentive but strict motherly love.

Human parents following the Polar Bear technique (assuming human Dad sticks around) generally have high expectations of their cubs, er, kids. There are household rules and enforced consequences for disobedience. The child's day is generally structured, and good behavior is expected and rewarded. Lines of communication between kid and parent are open, with lots of give-and-take. Parents explain the reasons for their expectations, and the child is raised to understand that she can speak to her parents without fear of harsh judgment or reprimand.

2. Harp Seals (dubbed "Neglectful" by psychologists)

Following an eleven-month pregnancy, Ma Harp Seal is a fairly dedicated parent for the first twelve days after birth. Then she pumps a flipper in the air, barks, "Okay, I'm done!" and finds better things to do, such as trolling singles bars for another mate. Ma Seal then leaves her baby stranded on the ice, where he learns to swim and hunt for food on his own. Or not. Thirty percent of harp seal pups die during their first year.

The human Harp Seal version of parenting produces children with a poor trust foundation because the parents take little interest in what's going on in their child's life and therefore don't meet the child's emotional, spiritual, and sometimes even physical needs. The home doesn't feel like a safe place for the child to share her life experiences and receive nurturing feedback, so she finds reasons to spend longer and longer periods of time away. The offspring of human Harp Seals often have a hard time forming relationships with other people and struggle with abandonment issues.

3. Black Eagles ("Permissive")

After the eggs hatch, Mom Black Eagle covers the basics, making sure the babies are fed and housed, but that's about all. She avoids confrontation and lacks the backbone to make and enforce rules in her own nest. She refuses to intervene in squabbles among her offspring and often just watches as her babies fight to the death. Can you say sibling rivalry on steroids?

Mom Black Eagle's human counterpart has difficulty setting limits for her children; she often compromises rules to avoid conflict. She may resort to bribery to entice her children to cooperate and would rather be her child's friend than parent. The child often ends up as an insecure, undisciplined, self-centered mini diva with poor social skills and a lack of motivation to improve.

We all know them, don't we? The out-of-control kid whom other mothers avoid inviting over to play because she systematically destroys all toys and property within her reach, while her own mom croons, "Oh, honey, you really shouldn't have ripped the head off Janie's new doll," or "Oops—was that a good choice, sweetie? You've ruined Miss Debbie's couch."

4. Orangutans ("Authoritarian" or "Obsessive")

Big Mama never lets her babies out of her sight. The original "helicopter mother," she obstinately hovers, supervising every move they make. She nurses them for six to seven years (fostering the longest dependency of any animal on earth). When the well dries up, males venture out on their own, but females stick with Big Mama for *ten years*, learning to use tools, build a sleeping nest, avoid predators, and everything else they need to know for homemaking and child-raising. Even after they're independent and leave the original family unit, girls frequently return to visit Big Mama. Those apron strings are springs forged from galvanized steel.

Actually, the hairy Big Mama (orangutan) is often more nurturing and compassionate than the traditional human "Authoritarian" hover-mom model. Although both Big Mamas lean toward obsession, the human version tends to coldly rely on punishment to enforce obedience to a list of strict rules. This Big Mama (or

Big Daddy) gives the child limited choices (if any), sees only black and white, and tends to resort to the can't-touch-this reason, "Because I said so!"

Big Mama's kids are prone to developing low self-esteem, hiding behind shyness, and exhibiting social ineptness. They often have difficulty thinking for themselves, harbor underlying resentment, and equate obedience with love. For example, I heard of one Big Mama household where faux presents bearing each child's name were placed underneath the Christmas tree. The kids thought they were real. Every time a kid misbehaved, Big Mama would toss one of their fake presents into the burning fireplace. You can bet those kids toed the line, but at what cost?

Please don't misunderstand—I'm not trying to condemn or advocate one type of parenting over another, just pointing out the differences. Your parenting style and choice of discipline are between you and Papa God. I only want to encourage you to prayerfully do your best to honor biblical principles and demonstrate to your children who is Lord of your life.

Listen, dear sister, if you take a long, hard, objective look at yourself and at your relationship with your child and don't like what you see, remember, it's not too late to make a change. It may take time. In point of fact, it *will* take time. . .but with diligence and Papa's strength infusing your own, it's entirely possible. Trust me, I know. I did it. (More about how to make simple but significant changes in the next chapter.)

I'm convinced that one of the keys to seeing discipline through to its positive end result is patience—something most mothers find in short supply because we've drained it searching for the sock mates that are somehow transported to the parallel universe where alien pogo children hop around on one foot. And discovering on the drive to school that Junior is responsible for two dozen cupcakes for the party *today.*

I have one word for you, girl: guppies.

Patience is something we do. We may not always *feel* patient, but we must *act* with patience. Surprisingly, the more patiently we respond to our children, the more patient we'll actually become. Even if we have to fake it at first. Like when we gather three barrels of clothes from the floor to wash, sort, and fold, only to find them again strewn on the floor the very next hour.

Now how did that slip through despite our "Train up a child in the way he should go" mantra? Who's training whom? Sometimes we're the ones wearing training pants.

So when patience is running low, fake it. Yes. Fake it. Pretend you're Noah's wife and you've just been sequestered on an ark with a gazillion animals and a shovel.

If all else fails, remember the countless times your heavenly Father has been patient with you. Emulate Him, so that one day your children will emulate Him too.

• •

Call them rules or call them limits. . .
they arc an expression of loving concern.
—Mr. Rogers

• •

Navigating the 'Hood

1. When was the last time you felt like a complete mom-failure? (If it was more than three hours ago, you get a tiara!)

2. Rarely do we fit completely into one single parenting style; we usually combine characteristics of several. For example, I'm an Orangupolartan (combination of Polar Bear and Orangutan). Which would you say you are and why?

3. Are you satisfied with the way your children are responding to your parenting techniques? Is there anything you feel led to change?

4. Patience is generally not the strong suit of *any* of us; we could all stand improvement. What are three practical things you can do to extend more patience toward your children?

CHAPTER 5

Prison Break

• •

Scaling My Fences

While they are still talking about their needs,
I will go ahead and answer their prayers!
ISAIAH 65:24 NLT

*P*assing by the state prison where Daddy worked, I used to stare up, up, up at those looming gun towers and impossibly high chain-link fences topped with razor wire, wondering how it felt to be trapped inside—to know that the big, wide world outside is rolling along, but you're stuck within these confining walls with no hope of escape.

Now, as a grown-up, I realize that sometimes we moms *do* feel imprisoned. Especially when we're

Physically exhausted (experiencing chronic fatigue)

Reduced to nagging (must repeat ourselves incessantly to be heard)

Invisible (underappreciated, taken for granted)

Sentenced to solitary confinement ("Am I the only one going through this?")

Off-kilter (having lost our spiritual balance; unable to hear Papa God's voice)

Nekked in front of a freight train (feeling helpless to change)

Yes, we do sometimes feel like prisoners. All that's missing are the baggy, striped pants. Hold on. Will you look at the striped sweats bedecking my southern hemisphere this very minute?

Well, sister-mom, I'm here to give you hope! You can break out of your prison. You are not stuck inside fences too high to scale. But you can't just sit there like a handful of linguini waiting for the pot to boil and magically transform you. You must do something different to make something different happen. Or this time next year you'll be in exactly the same place.

So stick your foot in the fence chink and start hoisting yourself up.

How, you ask?

A few small lifestyle redirections can make a huge difference. Since this is a book about mothering, let's first address the parenting perspective, and later we'll tackle the I-am-woman-hear-me-rip issues.

If there are parenting changes you need to make (and I'm guessing we all need to tweak our mothering skills occasionally), let's explore some simple, easy-to-implement solutions that can improve the physical, social, emotional, and spiritual health of your children.

Physical. Advances in technology have produced a generation of stagnant kids cemented to their (or their parents') electronic devices. Without the stimulation provided by physical activity (play) that helps develop gross motor coordination, improves nervous system function, builds muscle strength, increases stamina, burns excess energy, and controls weight, we end up with a bunch of tech-savvy marshmallows—smart, but weak and fluffy.

To balance the deficit, arrange physical activity for your child at least three times weekly. Whether it be hiking, biking, skating, participating in organized sports, or simply playing in a backyard or at a playground or park, get him off his duff and insist he move! If you can coordinate play time with other moms and kids, you'll earn bonus points in social and emotional development too.

Social. Electronic babysitting may have its place in certain (limited) circumstances, but chronic use of e-games, mind-numbing movies, and addictive social media produces kids who haven't a clue how to get along with others, show respect, share, be a gracious winner or loser, use good manners, or build others up ("Encourage one another and build each other up," 1 Thessalonians 5:11 NIV).

In short, they are ill-equipped to function in social situations. What's more, these clueless children become clueless grown-ups. Social skills are essential for becoming successful adults.

Sadly, because of our own excessive use of electronic devices, we moms may be unavailable to intervene and teach these crucial skills to our children. We're so preoccupied, we assume somehow they'll just figure it out on their own.

Um. . .nope. Just doesn't work that way.

Think of it like this: If you want little Edwina to learn how to brush her teeth, you have to teach her tooth-brushing skills. If you want Ralphie to pass on your prizewinning pineapple-walnut waffles to future generations, he must be instructed in how to make them. Likewise, if you want Lulabelle to be able to socialize, you must teach her social skills.

Make yourself available to impart socialization skills by spending face time together (and I don't mean the electronic kind): eat meals as a family; have tickle fests, pillow fights, or silly-string wars; designate a weekly family night (we claimed Friday nights as ours) and play interactive games like old-fashioned board games, cards (I'm Rummy Queen!), and outdoor flashlight Olympics. Do something fun together; laugh! Don't just sit and stare at each other (or a screen). The only use of electronics allowed during this time is the occasional family movie, but that should be only part of the evening's activities.

Make these happy romps a loving demonstration of how to honor Christ through interaction with others. Just be ready to toss in appropriate correction when your kids use each other as crash dummies.

Emotional. Not to beat a dead e-horse, but the artificial world created by electronics in which our children live supplies them with a false expectation that they must be constantly entertained. Studies reveal that technology overuse is rewiring our brains for chronic distraction.

In E-World, there are no quiet times. Bright lights and loud noise constantly bombard the senses; there are no boring times to perform real-life responsibilities like making beds, picking up toys, folding shirts, and other routine household chores.

It's all stimulation, action, and excitement. Not exactly like my real world—how about yours?

So naturally when we ask our kids to tear themselves away from E-World to peel carrots or empty trash cans, they kick like a mule with a sandspur up his rump.

Mother Teresa said, "We need to find God, and He cannot be found in noise and restlessness. God is the friend of silence."

It's important that we teach our kids to cultivate silence, productively fill their own "boring" downtimes, learn to wait, endure delayed gratification (you can't have everything you want *now*. . .flashbacks to Willy Wonka's obnoxious Veruca Salt), live in their own thoughts, problem-solve, nurture ideas, and hammer out personal beliefs—all necessary skills for functioning in the real world.

Many job tasks are repetitive, monotonous, even boring, yet will inevitably be involved in our kids' future vocation. (Can I get an amen from my sisters in the mom vocation who just finished washing, sorting, and putting away three loads of laundry?) So why not start teaching these skills while they're young?

We can start preparing our kids to creatively and productively cope with downtime by making some boring chores group projects with multiple family members participating together (for example, cleaning the house, washing cars, and preparing food).

While waiting in restaurants and medical offices, replace cell phones with simple, fun, quietly interactive games that strategically develop specific skills and require no special supplies or preplanning. Some of my personal faves: hangman (improves spelling) and tic-tac-toe (promotes strategy and logic)—both need only a pen and paper napkin. My peeps also love Twenty Questions (hones deduction skills), and for improving eye-hand coordination combined with a little friendly competition, try quarter soccer: face each other across a table and take turns flicking a sliding quarter in an attempt to balance it on the opponent's table edge without it falling off—she scores!

Delayed gratification can be taught by helping your child set goals and work toward them (for example, saving money for a new. . .um, unicycle) and by scheduling snack times (10:00 a.m. and 3:00 p.m. work for us) so they don't graze at will, developing an "If I want it, I'll take it" mindset. We really don't need a whole generation of Verucas, right?

According to Victoria Prooday, a pediatric occupational therapist (say, did you know I was an OT for thirty-six years?) with a decade of experience working with children and parents in establishing life skills, "To be able to delay gratification means to be able to function under stress. Our children are gradually becoming less equipped to deal with even minor stressors, which eventually become huge obstacles to their success in life. Make them wait; gradually increase the waiting time between 'I want' and 'I get.' "[1]

This, my resourceful mom-friend, is a proactive way to prepare your offspring for future workplace marketability plus teach them to be financially responsible and live within a budget.

Spiritual. If you recall, the *N* in our motherhood prison acronym stood for standing nekked in front of a freight train;

in other words, feeling vulnerable and completely helpless in the face of an unstoppable force about to mow you down. (By the way, *nekked* is quite different than *naked*; our Creator made us naked with beauty and dignity, but we make ourselves nekked through neglect and disrespect.)

Raising godly children in a world where spiritual warfare for their minds and souls is taking place on every plane of existence can feel pretty much like going nose to nose with a speeding freight train. But take this to heart, dear girl: we're not helpless. Not at all. There's something very real, very strong, and very proactive moms can do to defend and protect our precious children—we can pray.

Never, *ever* underestimate the power inherent in prayer. Praying is the most and the least we can do for these incredible beings who caused our hearts to leap outside our bodies when they were born and stay nestled in our arms ever after.

"What should I pray?" you may be wondering.

How about Hot Fudge Verses—scriptures we can pour over our children. We moms are more than willing to storm the fiery gates of hell to remind the hot mess with the proverbial pitchfork who our children *really* belong to. But the best way to storm the gates of hell is by storming the gates of heaven.

And which petitions could be more effective than those in the Word ordained by the Creator of the universe? "For the word of God is living and powerful, and sharper than any two-edged sword" (Hebrews 4:12 NKJV).

Please do make the time to compile your own go-to list of Hot Fudge Verses, but in the meantime, here are some of mine (remember, they're scriptures tailored as personalized prayers for each specific child):

𝓗𝓸𝓽 𝓙𝓾𝓭𝓰𝓮 𝓥𝓮𝓻𝓼𝓮𝓼

(to pour over your children and grands)

✳ Psalm 3:3 NIV: "You are a shield around [child's name]_____, O Lord; bestow glory on him/her [choose one], and lift up his/her head."

✳ Psalm 25:16–17 NASB: "Turn to _____ and be gracious to him/her, for he/she is lonely and afflicted. The troubles of his/her heart are enlarged; bring _____ out of his/her distresses."

✳ Psalm 71:3 NIV: "Be _____'s rock of refuge, to which he/she can always go; give the command to save him/her, for you are his/her rock and fortress."

✳ Psalm 91:11 MSG: "He ordered his angels to guard you, _____, wherever you go. If you stumble, they'll catch you; their job is to keep you from falling."

✳ Psalm 138:8 MSG: "Finish what you started in _____, GOD. Your love is eternal—don't quit on him/her now."

✳ Psalm 139:2–3, 7–10 NIV: "You know when _____ sits and rises; you perceive his/her thoughts from afar. You discern his/her going out and lying down; you are familiar with all his/her ways. . . . Where can _____ go from your Spirit? Where can he/she flee from your presence? If he/she goes up to the heavens, you are there; if he/she makes his/her bed in the depths, you are there. If he/she rises on the wings of the dawn, or settles on the far side of the sea, even there your hand will guide _____, your right hand will hold him/her fast."

So mom-friend, if you're feeling stuck behind towering brick walls topped with razor wire, don't despair. Grab your nail file. Time for a prison break!

• •

The only thing more terrifying than
screaming kids is silent ones.
—DEBORA M. COTY

• •

Navigating the 'Hood

1. When was the last time you felt incarcerated in motherhood prison? Which aspect of PRISON (the acronym) do you struggle with most?

2. What's not working as well as you had hoped in your current parenting lifestyle? Which of your children's— or your own—behaviors would you like to redirect? Brainstorm some ways you might accomplish this.

3. Which of the four life skill areas do you feel your family needs to focus on most at this time—physical, social, emotional, or spiritual? Why?

4. Do any of my Hot Fudge Verses resonate with you as a prayer for a specific child? Do any other scriptures come to mind that you can pour over your beloved in prayer? I strongly encourage you to create your own Hot Fudge list—the Psalms are a great place to start.

CHAPTER 6

I'll Pencil You In at 4:53

. . . .

Time Management

We can make our plans,
but the Lord determines our steps.
PROVERBS 16:9 NLT

I could feel her eyes boring into my back before I actually saw her. Oh man, not another interruption.

Sitting in my computer chair, as usual, I tapped away at keys that would hopefully forge my livelihood as a writer one day. I had such aspirations, such plans, such dreams.

But there stood my eleven-year-old daughter in the doorway of my "writing cave" (as she called it), drilling me with her death ray.

I stopped typing. My hands dropped to my lap.

After a moment of pregnant silence, a long, soft sigh resonated from Cricket's still-your-baby-but-not-for-long evolving form. In that sigh, I heard the sound of yearning, brimming with disappointment, choked with broken "I'll just be another minute" promises, missed mom-daughter adventures, and potential shared memories that had slipped forever away.

"I *hate* that computer," she uttered.

And the slender arrow of her longing pierced my soul.

What was I doing? I realized with sudden enlightenment that in order for my dreams to come true, I needed to wake up.

My eyes are leaking even as I'm writing this thirty years later. I'd blown it. I'd lost sight of what was most important. Notice I said *most* important; my writing career was certainly important, but it wasn't the *most* important. And as every mother knows, order of importance is crucial when you have finite time and limited energies.

I couldn't see it at the time, but I was permitting my own self-created agenda to ruthlessly rule my life, leaving no room for deviation from my tight, demanding schedule. Even at the expense of my greatest blessing—my family. "All the ways of a man are clean in his own sight, but the Lord weighs the motives" (Proverbs 16:2 NASB).

I'm here to tell you that Cricket's four simple words burned a hole in my focus fog, and by the Almighty's grace, I unscrewed my screwup.

Not that I was henceforth a perfect mother—far from it— but I began to order my priorities in a more God-pleasing way, which in turn increased my interruption tolerance and reduced my stress level, resulting in our family dynamics running oh, so much more smoothly.

Interruptions: the bane of a mother's existence. Can't finish one thing for ten others crammed into the overstuffed queue, often perpetrated by little people swarming around you like buzzing bees, thrusting their stingers into your last good nerve.

According to Dr. Sylvia Hart Frejd, life coach and author, "The unrest of human life comes largely from our being fragmented by so many disturbances."[1] *Unrest. . .fragmented. . .disturbed.* Yep. Those words pretty much describe an average mom-day, don't they?

Happily, there's something you can do about it. A scripture passage that enabled me to handle interruptions better—and I think it may help you too—was the story Jesus told in Luke 10:25–37. Take a moment to grab your Bible and refresh your memory. Especially this part (verses 33–35 NASB, emphasis mine):

> *But a Samaritan, who was on a journey, came upon him [the traveler beaten by robbers]; and when* he saw him, *he felt compassion, and* came to him *and bandaged up his wounds, pouring oil and wine on them; and he put him on his own beast, and brought him to an inn and* took care of him. *And on the next day, he took out two denarii and gave them to the innkeeper and said, 'Take care of him; and whatever more you spend, when I return* I will repay him.'

Remember, during this time in history, the Israelites despised the people from neighboring Samaria and avoided all contact with them, even crossing the road to walk on the opposite side. Samaritans were considered half-breeds and were often victims of racial prejudice.

Okay, let's look a little closer at the parts of this passage that relate to time management and interrupted schedules.

* *He saw him.* Compassion usually begins with the eyes; you can't care until you're aware. You must see—and often personally experience—a problem before your heart is engaged. Papa God has a way of using unscheduled, divine appointments (we call 'em interruptions) to divert our eyes from our relentless to-do list to what's really important.

* *He came to him.* It's easier *not* to help someone when you keep your distance. But once you open your mind to possibilities you haven't yet considered, you'll begin to feel the Holy Spirit's elbow jab of guidance. When He keeps poking at your spirit, it's time to step up to the plate, even if you left your best bat at another ballpark.

* *He took care of him.* The odds are slim that this dude was a career health care professional galloping off to a medical convention; he very likely had no more emergency wound care training than you or me, but he did the best he could with what he had. In *taking care* of this total stranger, he probably ripped up his own perfectly good clothing for bandages, used up his personal stash of wine for wound sterilization, drained his essential oils for healing, and willingly trudged the dusty road on foot so that the wounded man could have the choice seat atop his donkey, the ancient version of EMS.

✳ *I will repay you.* There's always a cost for kindness—are we willing to pay it? Might be money, time, energy, or worse yet, falling hopelessly behind on our tyrannical to-dos. The ultimate sacrifice.

Although he was hastening down the road with his own pressing agenda, the Samaritan stopped. He saw. He felt. He *allowed* himself to be interrupted for a greater cause. Hurry is a kindness-killer. In the words of Jerry McGregor, author of *40 Ways to Get Closer to God,* "Our challenge is to be open to serving others, not on our timetable, but theirs. Whether at home or work, be willing to see interruptions as opportunities to serve others. Consider it your mission to serve on this day. Don't tell anyone what you are doing, just serve them joyfully! And imagine that what you are doing for others you are doing for Jesus."[2]

You know, sister-mom, despite our meticulous planning (ha!), we never know when Papa has scheduled a divine appointment. . .a Holy Spirit–engineered encounter. . .an unforeseen brush with destiny.

Okay, let's be honest and call interruptions a pain in the royal rumpus—that's how you and I react, isn't it? With teeth gnashed and face grimaced. Because we don't like unexpected, unpredictable, unwelcome surprises. We want to do things our way, no muss, no fuss; we want to follow our carefully laid plans to predetermined outcomes.

When our plans are thwarted, our attitude drifts toward that of a two-year-old whose lollipop was hijacked by the rottweiler.

I'll admit I'm not a happy girl when my plans are impeded. I praise Jesus and stomp my foot at the same time. Why, oh why, can't I adapt to change more willingly?

Mostly because I'm just plain tired. Tapped out. Worn out. Mom-Mom-Mom-Mom'ed out. And that's when my interruption tolerance totally tanks and I tumble headfirst into the joy-sucking dully-funks.

You know the dully-funk pit all too well, girlfriend—you just didn't know what to call it. It's that black hole, when nothing particularly *bad* is happening, just nothing *good*. Our minds fog, our emotions go numb, our eyes glaze over, and we move like autotrons in a perpetual state of spiritual and emotional dullness.

A Mom'ed-out woman can spend days, weeks, even years in the joy-sucking dully-funks, functioning, going through the motions. . .taking care of her family, yes, but not really living life. She's barely eking by, persistently undone. Not experiencing the abundant life Jesus promised to believers in John 10:10 (NKJV): "I have come that they may have life, and that they may have it more abundantly."

The abundant life is like a Snickers bar—rich and satisfying. Is that how you'd describe your everyday life? If you're like me, you probably have an occasional rapturously abundant mom moment, but that feeling is hard to sustain. Why?

Because chronic fatigue tries to encase us in a rubber suit of apathy, whispering, "This will keep you safe. You can't be hurt if you don't care." So in self-protection mode, we muffle the barrage of emotions. We don't allow ourselves to *feel*.

But take care! That rubber suit will block Jesus-joy too. And happiness. And the exhilaration of feeling Papa God's pleasure in you—His beloved daughter. Apathy is a Son-block that numbs you to the wonder, excitement, and joy of living.

And that's a cocoon none of us wants to inhabit.

So how do we fit everything in one twenty-four-hour day and still reclaim ourselves? Probably not the way I did. When I hit fifty, I asked Papa God for more hours in the day to get everything done. He sent me menopause. Now I have half the stinkin' night too.

You've heard the old saying, "Water seeks its own level"? Well, I've got a time-management theory along similar lines. I call it the Bread Dough Rule. It goes like this: In the same way dough rises to fill whatever size bowl it's placed in, we fill our daily to-do bowl up to the brim, whether it's salad bowl sized or a mega mixing bowl.

So start with a pudding cup. Limit your must-dos today to three major items. You know good and well that the Bread Dough Rule will swell your list and overflow that tiny cup as the day progresses, but by starting small, you can afford unforeseen expansion and even—dare I say it?—hair-ripping interruptions.

So expect the unexpected today. And tomorrow. And the next day. Don't resent the interruptions; they're part of your Creator's to-do list for your life. (You thought *we* invented that idea? We were made in His image, you know!) Try to view them as opportunities to serve others. You *can* muddle through, and believe it or not, Papa God is standing by to bless your mess.

Hey, when your cup runneth over, sip from the saucer!

Make a list of important things to do today.
At the top of your list, put "eat chocolate."
Now, you'll get at least one thing done today.
—GINA HAYES

Navigating the 'Hood

1. I once jeopardized the thing most important to me in the whole world by allowing lesser priorities to crowd it out. What's most important to you, my friend?

2. What aspect of how the good Samaritan handled his major interruption resonated with you most? Which disruptions in your day tend to drive you batty?

3. Have you ever worn the self-protecting rubber suit of apathy? Are you wearing it now? How can you begin to remove this Son-block and experience more abundant life moments?

4. How does the Bread Dough Rule apply to your personal to-do list? What can you do to relieve the pressure of rising stress when you're Mom-Mom-Mom-Mom'ed out?

Section 2

· · · · · · · · · · · · · · · · · · ·

So Where's the Ding–Dang Motherhood Manual?

∽∾

*It's when you make yourself small
enough to fit into your child's world
that you're big enough to make an impact.*
—DEBORA M. COTY

You revive my drooping head.
PSALM 23:5 MSG

CHAPTER 7

Lipstick on a Pig

. . . .

Hidden Wounds

*God is our mighty fortress, always ready to help
in times of trouble. And so, we won't be afraid!*
PSALM 46:1–2 CEV

While visiting the Scottish highlands, the little mister and I came across some lovely, peaceful green moors. . .that happened to be disguising dangerous secrets. There's a good reason that sheep, thickly flocking every other edible field in the country, are nowhere to be seen on these particular moors.

The large expanses of seemingly innocent heather and sedge grasses conceal deadly peat bogs, or in Scottish Gaelic, quagmires.

Our tour guide explained that you could be hiking along, enjoying a pleasant moorland stroll, and suddenly come upon a wee sodden patch of sod camouflaged by brush. Another step and your boot would be sucked right off your foot. If you're a bit more unfortunate, your entire leg might sink into the quagmire, followed shortly by the rest of you, never to be seen again.

Traveling through quagmire-pocketed moors has always been hazardous; only during the past century was a dependable "floating" road finally devised for pedestrian and motorized traffic. Prior to that, I'm guessing many a hapless wanderer simply disappeared.

Also called "blanket bogs" because they cover the landscape like a blanket and are nearly invisible from a distance, these quagmires have collected quite an assortment of quarry over the centuries: wagons, livestock, provisions, stolen loot, murder weapons, and, sadly, all kinds of bodies, swallowed and preserved by the remarkable properties of sphagnum moss.

Some recovered victims had been tortured or killed before being thrown into the quagmire. Others appear to have met their fates after being accidentally sucked under. Regardless, Scottish moor travelers agree that it pays to be quagmire-educated and well prepared to avoid these covert threats.

We moms have hidden issues too—stressors not visible to others: festering wounds camouflaged by our everyday "game face," unresolved relationship rifts, consequences of poor choices, leftover childhood damage, gouges hacked by hurtful words, pain lingering beneath the surface, scars testifying to previous bloody encounters.

And they're not always physical scars, are they? Emotional scars can chafe, burn, and grind for decades, negatively affecting not only ourselves but our families as well. You think your peeps don't know about your hidden scars? Don't kid yourself. They do.

Hidden wounds are tough to heal because we tend to keep them covered rather than exposing them to light and air. But these wounds "need to breathe," as we tell our little one who wants to keep that grody superhero Band-Aid on his scraped knee for the tenth straight day. (Hey, aren't you glad there won't be any Band-Aids in heaven?)

In order for healing to take place, debris must be cleared away, the wound cleaned, healing balm applied, and sufficient time allowed for the protective scab to form and do its work. Wounds—and you get that I'm not just talking about physical wounds here, right?—must be attended, not ignored. If a wound is left unattended, the risk of infection increases and it may become septic. Even more painful. Crippling. Possibly deadly.

In my book *Fear, Faith, and a Fistful of Chocolate,* I share details about a hidden wound that was inflicted on me by someone I loved and trusted when I was twelve. I stuffed it deep inside, where it festered for forty years before finally being uncovered when a random comment by a childhood classmate inadvertently ripped off the Band-Aid.

It wasn't until my crusty, scabby, decades-old boo-boo was exposed to light and air that the healing process could be completed and I was able to resolve the secret fear that had affected my habits, choices, and behavior nearly my entire life.

So how do desperately driven moms go about ripping off nasty, old Band-Aids and exposing our oozing, pus-encrusted wounds to light and air? Here are a few doable suggestions from someone who's been there:

✳ *Nail it.* Identify the *real* problem. Are any of your current behaviors driving you nuts? Do they seem out of control or out in left field and you've no idea why you act this way? Perhaps it's yelling at your kids, snarking at Hubs, disrespecting your mother, flirting with a neighbor, pilfering supplies from work, habitually lying, stress eating, avoiding certain people like the plague. . .it could be any number of things. But listen, girlfriend—you're in good company. Even Jehovah's go-to guy, the apostle Paul, felt the same way: "When I want to do good, I don't. And when I try not to do wrong, I do it anyway" (Romans 7:19 NLT).

Raise your hand if this is you. Mine's up!

Now examine your past for clues to the source. Ask Papa God to guide you in sleuthing out and confronting the cause of your perplexing behavior (which, by the way, is merely a symptom of the underlying *real* problem). That's right—unearth and expose your wound. It might be buried layers deep.

On the other hand, you may already be well aware of that irritating emotional splinter beneath your middle fingernail, causing you to give everyone the finger, but you've put off doing anything about it. No more, my friend. Now's the time to grit your teeth and grab the tweezers.

✳ *Air it.* Have a heart-to-heart with Papa God. Admit your secret; wait for His response. "Cast your cares on the LORD and he will sustain you; he will never let the righteous fall" (Psalm 55:22 NIV). Believe me, you're going to get coated like a chocolate-dipped banana with the balm of grace.

Then confide in one or two trusted friends. . .not your entire women's roller derby team. Carefully select a safe place to store your secrets that you're confident won't spring a leak. Allow these soul sisters to help tug off that filthy, embedded bandage bit by bit. The act of uncovering (confessing) your hidden problem is the first step toward healing.

Meeting together weekly for several weeks (or longer)—say, over lattes—with BFFs (Blessed Friends Forever) who know the you beneath skin level can produce fresh insights and realistic approaches to dealing with the problem once and for all. Seeing a Christian counselor is always a good idea; many churches can recommend certified Christ-centered counselors who work on a sliding scale.

✳ *Bathe it in light.* If you don't have one already, invest in a thorough Bible concordance/reference book (you'll use this till your crow's-feet sprout wings, so get a good one) and several different Bible translations. My personal faves are the New King James Version (NKJV), the New American Standard Bible (NASB), and *NIV and The Message Parallel Study Bible*, which is a side-by-side comparison of the New International Version (NIV) and *The Message* (MSG). Consult your local Christian bookstore for other ideas.

Look up words or phrases related to your specific wound and do a personal Bible study (taking notes on passages and journaling your thoughts about what you're reading) on all related scripture, asking Jesus to reveal His-spective and initiate rehab from the inside out. Be prepared for enlightenment, because it's coming. Nothing is more eye-opening than pure Sonlight! "The righteous person may have many troubles, but the Lord delivers him from them all" (Psalm 34:19 NIV).

You know, sister, healing is a process; it can flow fluidly from start to finish or get stalled at any stage in between. For example, sometimes you may be dealing with scabs; at other times, scars. There's a difference.

Contrary to what your eyes tell you, scabs aren't a bad thing; although ugly and itchy, they're an integral part of wound protection during the healing process and hold the promise of full recovery if cared for properly. One day, you'll never know that disgusting scab was there.

Scars, however, never heal. They don't go away. We all have residual scars; some are connected with emotional baggage, some aren't, but they'll always be there to tell the tale. Scars—visible or not— are evidence of past trauma you've dealt with. . .yet survived.

Yes, you survived. And you will even again survive. Scars and all. That means Papa God wants you here—right where you are—because your life has meaning, worth, purpose. *His* purpose. He has His mighty hand extended to pull you out of the hopeless quagmire that seems to be pulling you under, so that you'll know despite your deepest, grossest, most putrefied wounds that His "power is strongest when you are weak" (2 Corinthians 12:9 CEV).

In the midst of uncovering a hidden wound of my own, I wrote this little poem about hope for complete healing in Christ. I pray that in some small way it will encourage you.

Renovator

Broken chair? The Carpenter can fix it.
Broken heart? The Carpenter can mend it.
Broken spirit? The Carpenter can restore it.
Broken life? Well. Maybe I should give Him a chance.
He is, after all, the reno Master.

In the lovely, lilting words of our Scottish guide regarding the hidden perils of quagmires, "Larn what treach'rous terrain looks like. If ye know what t' look fer, ye need fear n'moor."

And on the moors of life, we need fear no more either. As long as we know what to look for, we won't be sucked under.

• •

> *Being a mother is learning about strengths*
> *you didn't know you had, and dealing*
> *with fears you didn't know existed.*
> —LINDA WOOTEN

• •

Navigating the 'Hood

1. Do you struggle with any personal behaviors that embarrass you or your loved ones? Actions that you can't seem to explain? Befuddling thoughts that pop up from nowhere and affect your choices? How about destructive habits that feel out of control?

2. On a scale of 1 (low) to 10 (high), what number depicts your willingness to examine yourself for that elusive hidden wound? I'm hoping you've chosen 6 or higher; if so, will you commit to sit down this week and devise a workable plan to nail it, air it, and bathe it in light?

3. Are you aware of any partially healed wound lingering in your life that's still in the scab stage? What steps can you take to complete the healing process?

4. What are your thoughts about scabs versus scars? Which plague you most? You know, scars don't have to be considered hideous and shamefully hidden from view. Beauty truly *is* in the eye of the beholder. Don't you find the scars of your bestie beautiful, because the events that caused them molded her into the woman you love and admire today? Why not trust others to feel the same way about your scars?

CHAPTER 8

Thinking Outside the (Sand)Box

. . . .

Being Enough

I have loved you. . .with an everlasting love.
With unfailing love I have drawn you to myself.
JEREMIAH 31:3 NLT

*F*rank and Louie was an astoundingly ordinary cat. Yes,
you read that right; the cat was named Frank and Louie.
Can you imagine why? He passed away in 2014, but during
his fifteen years on earth, he was friendly, loving, and could
see two directions at once (every mother's dream, right?).

You see, Frank and Louie was a normal cat in every other
way, but he was born with two perpendicular faces (hence
the two names). Frank had his own nose and mouth, as did
Louie, but they shared two ears, three blue eyes, and one
large, fluffy cat body.

Say, do you suppose a two-faced cat eats twice as much?

Reckon he could meow a duet with himself? A little catnip probably goes a long way when you have two noses!

Frank and Louie was rescued as a newborn about to be euthanized. Janus kittens—a condition named for a Roman god with two faces—rarely live longer than a few days. But Frank and Louie decided that just wasn't good enough. He took matters into his own paws and became the longest surviving Janus cat in history. You go, boy! (Or is it boys?)

About that phrase, *good enough*. . . Do those two words rankle your deepest, darkest gut like they do mine? Sometimes it's not two-faced cats, but two-faced people who decide we're not good enough. Sometimes it's even us.

Especially when we're having one of *those* days, when mothering drains us dry. When lil' Princess Leia has a hysterical meltdown in the candy aisle, or Mama's boy Roy decides to taste-test his fresh nose pickings during the children's choir performance. Or drama queen Ilene screams with a vengeance those three heart-shattering words you never, ever, in a million years expected to hear: "I hate you!"

You're just *over* it.

Over your head.

Overcome.

Overdrawn.

Overrun.

Over-exhausted.

You're sure it's as obvious to everyone else as it is to you: you're just not good enough. Other moms don't seem to have these problems; they must be doing it right. Their kids don't flush the hamster down the toilet, bash the TV with a hockey stick, refuse to eat anything green except M&M's, tie the neighbor dog's legs together, wet their toothbrush without actually using it, and bathe only the "important parts."

Wait. Or do they?

I've got a newsflash for you, my kerfuffled friend: you're not the only one who thinks her maternal arrows are missing the bull's-eye. We *all* do. On some days—okay, *many* days—those arrows do fly willy-nilly, but it's okay. Hear me? I'll say it again: It's okay if you miss the target. Papa God created you to be enough for the specific needs of your children.

Even when you don't feel like it, it's still true: You. Are. Enough.

Now breathe. And try to relax a little. You're not ruining your kids any more than your parents ruined you by their parenting mistakes (no eye-rolling, please; I'm not finished). In fact, your heavenly Father spins many of those very mistakes to make you a better person and a better parent. Papa God is in the redemption business; He specializes in redeeming defective and damaged people.

When I look back on my childhood, I'm amazed I made it out alive. I recall many a balmy summer evening, asking permission to chase the town's mosquito-spray truck on my bike. My parents' casual, "Sure, why not?" permitted me to pedal into the thick fog of *poison* billowing out the back of the truck, filling my young, ignorant lungs with the equivalent of a gallon of Raid.

No doubt you remember similar circumstances from your past. So point made: every parent makes mistakes (more about this in chapter 11). No childhood is perfect. Yet children somehow live through them all the time and eventually become decent, law-abiding, God-honoring adults. Give it time to see how your mothering efforts will turn out, including the flawed ones.

Hey, flaws are not necessarily a bad thing—look at diamonds. They have flaws, and the inclusions (flaws) mark them as unique and belonging to a specific owner. The owner can claim that particular diamond as his own because of the flaws. Just as Papa God embraces ownership of us, His beloved mama-children, flaws and all.

So the next time you're embarrassed up the gazoo over your kids' incorrigible behavior, or feel shame over your mothering inadequacies, or writhe in guilt for, well, dang near *everything*, open up this little book and try thinking outside the (sand)box:

* *Surrounded by piles of stuff?* Offer a popcorn and movie date (with you) to each child who folds and puts away ten items of clothing. . .or toys. . .or school supplies (adjust the number to fit their ages). This is a win-win—you get cleaning help plus bonding time with your child; they get a fun "date" with Mom. You might even precede the movie with a pillow fight to harmlessly beat out some of your latent maniacal urges.

* *Can't hit the slam dunk?* Maybe your goal's too high. Perfection is still depicted in the media as something attainable, something others have but you don't. It's an illusion. Perfect moms and perfect children don't exist. My best advice for perfectionist moms is profoundly wise: Get over it. And repeat this crazed-mom creed every morning:

The Overachiever's Get-Over-It Creed

(based on Philippians 4:13)

"I can do all things through Christ"
Does not mean
I will do all things,
All at once,
All by myself,
All before the sun goes down.

＊ *Buried by bloopers?* Okay, girl, stop counting your failures and ignoring your successes. Think of three good mothering things you did today (yes, you may include feeding them, clothing them, and driving them to soccer, even if it was three bowls of Froot Loops, her shirt was on backwards, and you forgot his cleats). Hey, just keeping them alive one more day gets you a gold star.

If you can't dredge up three, make something good happen before the day is over. With apologies to my health-food BFFs, how about a little fudge-making fellowship with the kiddos after dinner? Or doughnuts—my kids had a blast when we made homemade doughnuts together by cutting the centers out of canned biscuit dough with a small round spice jar lid, fried the doughnuts and holes in cooking oil, then dropped them into a brown paper bag containing powdered sugar. They took turns shaking the bag until the luscious, finger-lickin' doughnuts were removed, cooled, and scarfed. But not necessarily in that order. *Mmm.* Happy food memories last forever.

✳ *Too many Momzilla moments?* When your inner beast busts out of its cage, it's time for a self-safari. *Before* your fam hauls out the tranquilizer rifle. Incessantly picking at kids or the hubster usually means you need a break, sweetie. It's not optional. You *must* step away and regroup. Fatigue is one of women's biggest production-killers and relationship-damagers. You may protest that because you're not good enough, you don't deserve a break (gotta keep trudging along to get it all done), but you'd be dead wrong. Or maybe just dead.

Rest is a basic need of Momzillas, as important as breathing in and out all day. So step outside and wipe off the porch swing; water some plants; pull a few weeds. Or better yet, just pretend to do those things. Sit and stare at a tree if it won't guilt you too much. Stretch. Release tension. Unwind. Close your eyes for a happy nap. You know it's true: when Momzilla misses her nappy, ain't nobody happy!

✳ *Lost your laugh?* I so get that. I felt the same way as a young mother. It's hard to remember what carefree mirth feels like when you're wrestling a stuffed bunny out of the clogged toilet, scrubbing dried pizza from the carpet, or witnessing the baby consume a steady diet of bugs, dog food, and plastic grapes. But take heart—this kind of craziness only lasts a season. A limited time. Trust me, it's true. May not feel like it right now, but it won't be this way forever. Better times, they are a-coming.

In the words of mom-blogger Sarah Sandifer, "There are going to be a few years when they have all of you, every ounce of your strength and every shred of your energy. There's going to be a time when they lay claim to your patience, your sanity, your everything. That's just how it has to be for a bit. They need your strength until they can find their own."[1]

So how do you reconnect with your lost laugh during these wrung-out years? Try doing something unexpected and outrageous. Put on crazy music and wear underpants on your head; have a family dance-off and crown a dancing queen/king; climb a tree with your kids; run through an open field flying a kite; have an Easter egg hunt with kumquats in July. . . . The sky's the limit. The happiest times accrue while cavorting with your kids.

Some days I wish I were like Frank and Louie, but in addition to twice as many visual fields of kid-supervision, I'd like twice as many hands. Just think—I could accomplish twice as much in an hour! But then again, with two mouths chomping away and four hands shoveling in Cadbury, I'd weigh twice as much. *Ugh*.

I think I'll stick with little ol' me, just the way I am. Because I. Am. Enough.

• •

Don't cry because it's over.
Smile because it happened.
—DR. SEUSS

• •

Navigating the 'Hood

1. Do you wrestle with feelings of not being good enough as a mother? As a woman? In which areas do you feel inadequate? What factors do you think may have contributed to your feeling this way?

2. What has been your childrearing experience with my Theory of Negative Relative-osity? It states: As soon as you utter, "My child will *never. . .*" cosmic forces kick in to ensure that your little darlin' will perform that precise behavior for the rest of his life. Or until you end his life (remember those guppies!).

3. What circumstances tend to bring out the Momzilla in you? Brainstorm three ideas for how to avoid those circumstances and keep that runaway monster muzzled and caged.

4. Which of my suggestions for thinking outside the (sand) box resonates most with you? How might you be able to incorporate it into your mom-life?

CHAPTER 9

Becoming You-Nique

. . . .

Finding My Mothering Niche

The tongue can kill or nourish life.
PROVERBS 18:21 NLT

I'll never forget the day my son disappeared. Matthew, just shy of two, was an inquisitive, wiggly toddler, too smart for his own britches, as my granny used to say.

I'd mustered my courage and ventured into the mall's most upscale boutique searching for a special-occasion dress. It was foreign turf compared to my usual discount department store haunts. I don't know what possessed me to go in; I couldn't afford anything. Just dreaming, I suppose, as wistful gals submerged in diapers tend to do.

As I perused out-of-my-league dresses with one hand while pushing Matthew's stroller back and forth with the other, I suddenly realized I was shoving an empty stroller. The seat belt was securely buckled around. . .air.

I hit the floor commando style, scrunching beneath racks of overpriced clothing, peering into corners, searching high and low for my vanished progeny.

Suddenly two high-heeled feet parked themselves mere inches from my nose.

"May I help you, madam?" asked a silken voice from above. As she lowered herself to my level—as if that were possible—I noticed her name tag: Ms. Hightower, Manager (name changed to protect the snooty).

Uh-oh. Busted.

Scrambling to my feet, I tugged my Elmo sweatshirt down and my Walmart jeans up. "Oh, no, ma'am. Actually, yes. . .well. . .maybe," I stammered, completely flustered. "I've lost something. Actually, it's more like some*one*—"

Just then, laughter erupted from a growing group of mall shoppers gathered in front of the boutique's display window. My gaze followed their pointing fingers to a blond mannequin seated on a low stage, her arms raised in frozen festivity, colored hose stretching from the tip of each extended finger to form a multihued rainbow extending to the ceiling.

There, in the blond lady's lap, sat my prodigal son, his chubby arm wrapped around her stiff neck, her curly wig askew over one eye. Little Houdini giggled gleefully as he smashed his cookie against her painted lips.

I dashed toward the display window, a surprisingly fleet Ms. Hightower right on my heels, her perfectly waxed eyebrows now arching in horror, the faux blush on her cheeks distinct round splotches like strawberries in a bowl of cream.

"Matthew, come to Mommy. . .*now*!" I called through the toddler-sized slit created by a locked sliding panel. Matthew's growing audience chortled in delight as he poked his new friend and declared, "Oooh, Mommy! Look—pretty lady!"

I realized that a toddler with groupies was not going to be reasonable, so I shoved my arm into the small opening and managed to snag the toe of his sneaker. I began reeling him in, inch by inch, with loudly protesting Matthew dragging the petrified lady along for the ride. The colored hose attached to her fingertips popped loose from the ceiling like rogue gunshots. The crowd roared.

I finally managed to wedge my squirming son through the hole; Matthew emerged clutching a dismembered plastic arm bearing the remnants of shredded stockings. Wrestling the severed appendage from his tiny iron grip, I handed it to an openmouthed Ms. Hightower, muttered a mortified, "I'm *sooo* sorry," and fled the crime scene with Matthew howling in his getaway stroller.

I never stepped foot in that mall again without a hat and sunglasses.

Sigh. I know. You know.

You too have cried, "You're killin' me, Junior!" after one too many peeing-on-the-neighbor's-prize-gardenias incidents.

Well, I've got terrific news! New scientific studies have found that having children actually *extends* your life.[1] No kidding—people with kids can expect to live one to two years longer than those without. Go figure. Maybe Papa's making up for all the lost time when we couldn't manage to shave our faux-woodchuck legs.

It's nice to know that parenting has at least one dividend; many days, all you can see are liabilities.

Like when your five-year-old locks you and your two toddlers in the upstairs bedroom— phoneless, of course—for three hours in the middle of the day and your only hope of escape is to hang out the window hollering your house alarm code to the (male) neighbor you've never met, while begging him to wade through the toy battlefield that's your house and spring you. (Thanks for sharing this mom-cringe story, Carly!)

Or when you're nailing your errant kid with a steely glare and reaching for the dreaded flip-flop for the tenth time in one day.

What? You don't ascribe to the projectile flip-flop disciplinary technique (a rogue parenting style holdover from chapter 4)? I know my Latina chicas do; they call them chanclas, which is translated "slippers" or "flip-flops," a word that strikes fear and trembling into the hearts of naughty children of all ages.

I learned this weapon of sass destruction from my aforementioned granny, who wasn't Hispanic, but backwoods-make-you-panic. Granny's aim rivaled that of any major league baseball pitcher. Whether thrown or applied manually, slippers left indelible marks on my childhood. And they weren't just utilized by relatives either; all naughty heinies or flailing limbs were fair game, regardless of who you belonged to.

Trample a neighbor's begonia while playing chase, or break a flower pot with a carelessly thrown ball, or maybe let your sassy mouth run away from you, and—*whack!*—off comes the slipper with lightning speed and you simply cannot *believe* the agility with which that little white-haired lady chases you down and applies the sole of chastening.

Mouth shut. Lesson learned. Never again.

Memories are strong enforcers. I've seen YouTube videos of grown men—big, burly, macho men—blanching and cowering in fear at the glimpse of a tiny, shriveled-up grandma reaching for her shoe. It's been known to send hardened criminals running for cover, screaming, "I'm sorry! I'm sorry! I won't do it again."

You know, maybe we should incorporate this effective form of punishment for wrongdoing into our courts of law. We could replace dignified, robed judges with angry grandmas wielding blazing slippers. We might actually deter future crimes if aspiring criminals knew they'd have to face *The Shoe*.

Okay, so I won't hold it against you if projectile flip-flops aren't your disciplinary thing (by the way, the technique works wonderfully with pets too; my poodle freezes in mid-naughtiness when he sees my hand make a move toward my flop). Our enforcement strategies certainly aren't all the same. Why, you may have never poured a glass of ice water over your teenage son's head when he smarted off at the dinner table either, but I promise I'll not dis you. As I mentioned in chapter 4, we each have to find our own mothering niche.

The truth is, there's no one best way to parent; each child is different and each mom is different. If there was a single "right way," everybody would be doing it.

I hope none of us are pompous enough to believe we've got it right and everybody who disagrees with us is wrong. As we discussed in chapter 1, our only example of the perfect parent is Papa God. And the way He responds to us—His children— when we sin is the way we should respond to our own children when they blow it: "GOD is sheer mercy and grace; not easily angered, he's rich in love. He doesn't endlessly nag and scold, nor hold grudges forever. He doesn't treat us as our sins deserve, nor pay us back in full for our wrongs" (Psalm 103:8–10 MSG).

Let's take a closer look at our heavenly Father's preferred parenting qualities from this passage:

* Shows mercy

* Extends grace

* Is not easily angered

* Loves generously

* Doesn't endlessly nag and scold

* Doesn't hold grudges forever

* Doesn't deal out justice unmercifully

* Doesn't exact revenge

Wow. I don't think this checklist describes me even on a good day. . .but I'd sure like for it to. I aspire to parent my children (and grandchildren) more like my heavenly Father parents me. Even if flying flops and surprise dinner-table showers don't always fit that model. Thankfully, no behavior is permanent. If it's learned, it can be unlearned, right?

Sometimes we have to backpedal a bit in order to finally move forward.

I know. I look tired. But I have kids.
I'm pretty sure this is just my face now.
—MEME SMACK

Navigating the 'Hood

1. Can you recall an incident when you were sure your kids were sending you to an early grave? Or maybe you *wished* they were so you could escape embarrassment?

2. Were there any particular weapons of sass destruction from your childhood that you carried over into your parenting?

3. Flip back to the list of Papa God's preferred parenting qualities; review them slowly and thoughtfully, pausing at each one to consider how that quality has (or could have) played out in specific real-life instances with your kids.

4. How do you stack up against your heavenly Father's standard of parenting? Which of the parenting qualities can you check off the list? Which do you feel you need to work on more?

CHAPTER 10

Blabber Control Issues

. . . .

Sometimes Ya Just Gotta Laugh

If we are "out of our mind" as some say, it is for God.
2 CORINTHIANS 5:13 NIV

*A*dmit it, girlfriend, sometimes you just lose it. Your
emotional grip, I mean. Can't really explain why; you're
limping along holding it all together—barely—when some
seemingly insignificant thing hurls you over the cliff. You
recklessly let loose on anybody and anything (not necessarily
human) within screaming distance.

Spouse ducks into the linen closet, kiddos fly to their
rooms, your mother hangs up to run an errand she suddenly
remembers, the quivering dog dives beneath the couch, the
cat looks like she stuck her paw in a light socket.

What in the world happened? You don't have a clue.
Something inside snapped.

When the spittle settles, you're ashamed. And oh-so-remorseful. Listen, I'm not saying it's okay to blast away with your blazing Uzi tongue, but it *is* normal to reach a breaking point. All moms do.

Mounting stress builds pressure in the reservoir until one more tiny drop bursts the dam and we freak. Sort of like the cranky croc at the Australian Reptile Park who totally lost it when a noisy mower sent him over the edge. You'll love this (true) story.

Shortly after the zookeeper began tending the lawn in the large reptile enclosure (as he had previously done numerous times without mishap), something inexplicably lit a fire under Elvis, a sixteen-foot, 1,100-pound crocodile. (Maybe Elvis was trying to take a nap; I get awfully testy when my neighbor mows during my naptime too.)

So Elvis took off after the worker, repeatedly lunging at the poor guy as he fended off the enormous reptile with his mower (okay, I might've done this with my neighbor a few times too). Elvis grabbed the 100-pound push mower between his razor-sharp teeth, waved it above his spiny head, then dragged it underwater, breaking two teeth in the process.

Evidently a grudge-holder, Elvis grumpily guarded his booty all day. That's right—Elvis would not leave the enclosure. Nor would he allow anyone close enough to recover the waterlogged mower until he was lured to the other end of the lagoon with a tasty treat. Hey, I can relate; grumpy or not, I'd go anywhere for a hot fudge sundae with nuts.

That day, the straw that broke the camel's back was the mower that broke the croc's tooth.

We all have our own version of Elvis's mower—our customized dam-burster. The just-one-more brownie that plings the skirt button across the room. The stomping-on-my-last-nerve incident that triggers a shocking, out-of-control tirade that reminds us we haven't dealt with our blabber control issues.

Thanks to raging pregnancy hormones, unexplainable mom-behavior often begins even before our offspring arrives. Experts benignly call them "nesting instincts" or "prenatal urges," but you and I know they're mad, irrepressible obsessions that simply will not be ignored. Some make a modicum of sense, like feeling that you *must* remodel the kitchen and/or bathroom before Baby arrives (thanks for sharing your nesting stories with me, Kitty, Sam, Veta, Kristi); or creating pre-scrapbook pages for newborn pictures (Pamela); or repairing, waxing, and detailing the car for Baby's first ride (Betty, Sue, Season).

But then there are quirky, irrational obsessions that seize our minds, like endlessly scrubbing and sanitizing floors, toilets, or trash cans (Yvonne, Karen, Kim); relentlessly searching for a glass-breaking tool to get the children out of the car in case it falls off a bridge into a river (Wendy); repainting perfectly decent walls for no reason except you just *have to* (Kat).

Of course, there's also washing, organizing, and then rewashing and reorganizing all of Baby's clothes (Jen); insisting that Hubs moves your two-ton bed so that every last cat hair can be vacuumed in case your newborn decides to hang out behind the bed (Debbie); dragging your rotund self to the mall to buy baby shoes because of recurrent nightmares that your (nonwalking) infant will be terrifyingly shoeless (Elizabeth).

Or perhaps taking down all your blinds during your ninth

month and dragging them into the yard to scrub in a washtub (Judy); waiting until you go into labor to wash the bathroom rugs so they'll be clean and fluffy for Baby—as if he'll notice (Leondra); and my personal fave, climbing up on a tractor to mow ten acres the day before you give birth (Karen).

Yep, no one *makes* moms do these things. We just know they have to be done. Period. Don't argue. End of discussion.

I wonder if our Master Designer had a mischievous grin on His big, beautiful face when He doled out those wacky hormones that run amok for nine months prior to giving birth and then monthly thereafter until the grands come along.

One thing I do know: Papa God has a wonderful sense of humor, and He loves it when we laugh. I believe laughter is the best salve for the skinned knees of the spirit. And heaven only knows how many times we'll skin who knows what before this mom gig is over.

One of the ironies of motherhood is that you do so, so much, but you always think you should be doing more. In the throes of exhaustion, your will can sometimes write a check that your body cannot cash. To avoid mommy crash-and-burn, you need a break. . .a diversion. . .a pause that refreshes.

So for your giggling pleasure, I've compiled some of my own hilarious kid-gems and those I've collected from reader BFFs. I hope you'll send me yours too—never can tell where your story may pop up!

* When trying to explain Matthew 7:12 in six-year-old kid-speak, my friend Debbie came up with, "Jesus tells us that we should treat others as we would like them to treat us. If you would not want someone to call you poopy-face, you should not call anyone else poopy-face."

* A distraught little boy ran up to Karen, a teacher, on the playground, pointed to some big kids playing nearby, and wailed, "They're saying God's name in cursive!"

* While grousing about our alien teens, my friend Cheryl lamented, "If only we could freeze-dry our kids until they're twenty-five and then add water."

* Young Ella wasn't sure what a secretary did when she was coerced into running for the office in her sixth-grade class. After the first official meeting, Ella was asked where the minutes were. She pointed to her watch.

* After a fifth-grade Bible lesson on the eighth chapter of Acts, Ryan went home and told his parents that God must allow animals in heaven; Philip baptized a unicorn. (Hey, I shall not be a bit surprised if the pearly gates have a pet door!)

* Joey the college freshman was sure surprised when he opened the large package from his mom; it was the trash he'd forgotten to take out while he was home for the weekend.

* Little Ruthie kept inching down the church pew, crowding her mother. "What are you doing?" Mom whispered. "That man"—Ruthie tilted her head toward the elderly man sitting a few feet away—"smells like he rolled in a dead possum on the way to church."

* During her pregnancy, Charmaine had a recurring dream that making babies is like making cakes; you walk along a massive shelf and choose your ingredients

(gender, race, eye color, freckles, hair texture, etc.), blend them together and pour the batter into a baby-shaped pan, pop it in the Almighty's big oven, and—voilà—out comes your lil' dickens.

✳ Cindy, a third-grade Sunday school teacher, overheard little Jenna bragging about her new Bible: "It's NIV!" she said proudly. "What does that mean?" another girl asked. "Um. . ." Fleeting puzzlement crossed Jenna's face, but then she replied confidently, "It's the New Intestinal Version!" Cindy couldn't help but ask if it was the large or small intestinal version.

✳ Some insightful bits of biblical trivia I've gleaned from kids during my forty years in children's ministry:

a) Noah's floating arcade landed on Mt. Thermostat.
b) God wrote on aspirin tablets for Moses and the ten commandos up on Mt. Cyanide.
c) One hysterical (historical) Bible action figure is Solar-man (Solomon), who kept very busy with seven hundred wives and three hundred porcupines.
d) A concubine is a machine that harvests corn on a farm.

Are you grinning yet, sister-mom? Just to make sure, I'm closing this chapter with the best blabber-control story *ever*!

When my kiddos were young, we attended a small church that didn't have children's church, so after the age of five, kids went into big church with their parents. One day I noticed six-year-old Cricket doodling on her bulletin, daydreaming, and muttering to herself during the sermon.

So the next Sunday morning in the car on the way to church, I gave her the "You're a big girl now and therefore must learn to listen to the preacher" lecture. We arrived to find a very stern, ultra-regal, black-robed visiting minister filling in for our own laid-back, easygoing pastor.

My wide-eyed daughter was plastered against the back of her chair as the heavy-winded minister bellowed the scripture reading. Then during the offertory, he lifted his hands toward heaven and prayed in a pious tone, "Lord, without you, we are but dust. . ."

My precious dumplin'—who was *listening!*—piped up in her little-girl voice loud enough to bring the whole service to a chuckling halt: "Mommy, what is *butt dust*?"

* *

Parenting is a delicate balance of convincing your child they can do anything in life while simultaneously screaming, "Don't do that!" every three minutes.
—A TUNED-IN DADDY

* *

Navigating the 'Hood

1. Who or what usually receives the brunt of your out-of-control tirades? Have you ever picked up a lawn mower with your teeth like Elvis?

2. Does your will ever write a check your body cannot cash? How do you deal with mommy crash-and-burn? How does your fam handle it?

3. Which of my kid-gems is your favorite? Which of your own?

4. Ever consider journaling? I highly recommend it. Pause right now to jot down a few of your own kid-gems before you forget and they're forever lost.

CHAPTER 11

Too Blessed to be Obsessed

. . . .

Letting Go of Mom-Guilt

*The more words you speak, the less
they mean. So why overdo it?*
ECCLESIASTES 6:11 NLT

*W*e all have 'em: those what-in-the-world-was-I-thinking
parenting blunders that haunt us.

I could make your hair stand up with a few of my doozies,
but my gold-medal mess-up occurred the year Cricket was
seven and struggling with separation anxiety. Actually, she'd
always had a hard time letting Chuck and me out of her sight
(she was the church nursery toddler who never stopped crying),
but that spring she was exceptionally clingy, wrapping herself
around my leg at school drop-off and howling like a banshee
when I peeled her off.

So when summer finally rolled around, I was utterly

exhausted and more than ready for a break as we took off for our annual Daytona Beach week with extended family.

Cricket and Matthew (older by almost three years) were having a blast playing with their cousins when Chuck and I learned we'd need to leave three days early to take care of something important at home. My parents and sister graciously offered to keep our kids at the beach and drive them home at the end of the week.

Well, to me the prospect of three whole days of grown-up time sounded like absolute paradise—a no-brainer. We knew Matthew would be fine, but the problem was how to get away without igniting a nuclear Cricket explosion.

It was at that point I made one of the worst parenting decisions of my life. The solution seemed simple: disappear. We wouldn't tell her we were going. No messy, extended good-byes; no slobbering, screeching protests; no desperate little hands clutching, clutching, clutching. Just. . .*poof*. Gone.

Surrounded by family she knew and loved, she'd get over it, right? Sure.

So we packed our bags and snuck them into the car. Then when Cricket and her cousins were playing in a back room, we quietly slunk out and drove away.

Ah, such freedom! Chuck and I turned off our phones to avoid any interruption of our newfound peace and were almost giddy with relief on the three-hour drive home. It wasn't until we walked into the too-quiet house and I saw Cricket's loved-to-tatters teddy bear lying forlornly on the couch that I started to feel the full impact of what I'd done.

I had abandoned my daughter. I'd left her without any

explanation, without any assurance of my love. I had forsaken her trust and disregarded her needs, thinking only of my own.

The next three days were a blur of tears and guilt amid excruciating phone reports of an inconsolable little girl sitting all by herself—mourning—while the other children played and swam. She wouldn't eat and cried herself to sleep every night. Too young and immature to understand why we had left, but old enough to feel deserted by the two people she trusted most. Her little world crumbled.

Guilt flattened me like a steam iron.

Tell me, why is mom-guilt a step beyond regular guilt on the suffering scale? I dunno—maybe it's because we've been entrusted to love and protect these precious little people who bear our crooked noses and knobby knees, and when we bungle that sacred responsibility, we set ourselves up as sitting ducks for flaming guilt arrows shot straight from the pit of hell.

Satan's full-time job is to accuse us; the Accuser (Revelation 12:10) takes his job very seriously. We must be alert and aware of his covert agenda—to pelt us with sizzling guilt until we're worthless blobs of misery, paralyzed by blame, doubt, and guilt, deplorable especially to ourselves.

Listen, sister-mom, let's not blob up. Nor plaster targets to our chests. Instead, let's don the armor of God (see Ephesians 6:10–18) to deflect those flaming arrows and evade the insidious guilt that engulfs our spirits like wildfire.

I once heard a British rector in London quote wise old theologian Charles Spurgeon, "The devil never kicks a dead horse." Nope. That's because it's a useless waste of evil energy; the dead feel nothing. They're already spiritually impotent.

The devil only goes after those who are a vigorous threat—those who are alive and animated in Christ and thereby a roadblock to Satan's goal of neutralizing Jesus-joy in the lives of those whom Papa God has designated as faith mentors to the next generation: *moms.*

That's you. That's me.

And hitting us in the emotions is an effective way to debilitate us.

Blogger Elizabeth Hoagland says it best: "Guilt is not from God; the Holy Spirit may *convict* us of something, but shame and blame are Satan's game."[1] And shame and blame are no lightweights; they weigh us down like a suitcase full of rocks.

Dragging around that heavy guilt baggage, we often feel defeated before we can even start unpacking. What to do? How to unload? Where to begin? Well, if you'd like to dump the hefty trunk you're carrying right now, here are some ideas:

❊ *Buddy up.* Recognize that you're not the only one lugging those overloaded bags around the airport. It's time to approach the help desk, where you'll find empathy and support. Find or form a Bible study or support group of sister-moms; you don't have to navigate this journey alone. "Resist him [the devil], standing firm in the faith, because you know that your brothers [and sisters] throughout the world are undergoing the same kind of sufferings" (1 Peter 5:9 NIV).

❊ *Label your baggage, then lose it.* Yep, claim it, name it, then chuck it. Identify what's weighing you down. Mom-guilt has many subgroups, you know: nursing versus non, working versus stay-at-home, daycare choice, mode of discipline, DIY remorse ("I should've made his costume instead of buying it"), Pinterest inadequacy ("Why can't I do all this too?"), birthday party inferiority (if you spent more than $50 on your kid's last birthday party, you know exactly what I mean), and pressure to join (groups/lessons/clubs), to name a few. We even view our child's sports performance and academic achievement as reflections of our mothering. As if it's our fault he struck out every single at-bat and she made a C+ on the test when Darlin' Darla next door made an A. (Betcha Darla's mom hired a tutor!)

So give it some thought—writing it out is even better—and name every specific mothering guilt that's oppressing you; hold each weighty rock in your hands. Own it. Ask forgiveness if need be. Then drop it like a hot potato. Let it go. Because even sweet potatoes (good moms) explode when they're nuked too long.

Believe me, dropping those rocks is a *huge* relief. Now leave 'em down there; do *not* pick them back up. What's done is done; you can't undo it any more than I can go back in time and *not* walk out on my little girl. But hear this: Papa God can redeem our poor mom-choices.

Holocaust survivor and my personal spiritual hero Corrie ten Boom said, "When we confess our sins, God casts them into the deepest ocean, gone forever. . . . Then God places a sign out there that says 'No Fishing Allowed!'"

So stand up straight. Step away from that pile of rocks. Shout, "Woo-hoo!" You get to start over. All because of God's grace. "And the God of all grace, who called you to his eternal glory in Christ, after you have suffered a little while, will himself restore you and make you strong, firm and steadfast" (1 Peter 5:10 NIV).

✳ *Repack.* Lighter this time; you're allowed only one carry-on. No rocks, not even pebbles. That means disqualifying yourself from the Accuser's shame and blame game. Remember, Satan—also called the father of lies (John 8:44)—is clever, for there's often a snippet of truth in his accusations, just enough to riddle you with doubt. And a partial lie is tougher to combat than a blatant lie. Learn to discern.

✳ *Shake the mental Etch A Sketch.* Don't be conformed to the world's standards; shun the impossible mother image the world projects. Who said you have to be Supermom to prove your worth? Certainly not your Master! He doesn't ask for perfection; He asks for humility. And if you've been a mama for more than one day, you've got plenty of that. "Don't copy the behavior and customs of this world, but let God transform you into a new person by changing the way you think. Then you will know what God wants you to do, and you will know how good and pleasing and perfect his will really is" (Romans 12:2 NLT).

So let's agree that we all make mothering faux pas. Some small, some humongous—as in abandoning your seven-year-old. But our blunders are redeemable if we give our rock pile to the Lord and view reflexive guilt as an indicator of how deeply we care about our kids, rather than an incriminating neon finger flashing over our heads, *Bad Mom. . .Bad Mom. . .Bad Mom.*

Our past mistakes can crush us beneath their oppressive rock-weight, or they can sharpen us into a better mother for tomorrow. I choose option B, don't you? So let's stop looking back. When we stay riveted to life's rearview mirror, we miss the horizon of hope in front of us, painting the future fifteen incredible shades of pink.

• •

A mother's love is unconditional.
Her temper is another subject.
—SMARTY-PANTS KID

• •

Navigating the 'Hood

1. What would you consider the gold-medal mess-up in your mothering history? How was it resolved? (By the way, it took time and intentional effort to reestablish trust with my daughter after the beach abandonment incident, but Papa turned it into a "redeemable blunder" and our relationship was eventually fully restored. I consider that she chooses to live next door today as a big YAY for Papa God!)

2. Is it hard for you to admit your parenting mistakes? Why do you think that is?

3. How do you deal with your mom-guilt? Ignore it? Keep a secret collection? Beat yourself up on a regular basis? How would you *like* to deal with your mom-guilt?

4. Are you dragging around any guilt rocks in your luggage today? Examine the four baggage-dumping suggestions in this chapter; how does each one relate to you? Which are you doing already? Which would you like to begin?

CHAPTER 12

Chocolate Caulks Relationship Cracks

. . . .

Forgiveness

Don't insist on getting even; that's not for you to do.
"I'll do the judging," says God. "I'll take care of it."
ROMANS 12:19 MSG

One summer day I was taking a walk in beautiful West Chester, Pennsylvania, and came upon a sign in front of a Quaker school that read "Friends Public Shredding This Saturday."

Appalled, I did a double take. *What?* Since when did we start shredding our friends in public? My goodness, it's bad enough that we do it in private.

Someone gently explained (with no small amusement at my horrendous misinterpretation of the sign) that this gathering was to shred expired documents as a community service offered by the "Friends" (another name for Quakers).

Um. . .oh.

Sadly, my ignorant assumption was based on my personal experience of—far too often, I'm afraid—witnessing friends verbally shred other friends.

You've seen it too. You may have actually been the one shredded. I know I have. When that happens, our hearts become calloused with thick, self-protective gristle, which blocks further hurt from penetrating. But it also hinders outgoing Christ-generated emotions like compassion and mercy. We become numb, dumb, and dense. As dynamic as a fence post.

Perhaps we haven't a clue how to dissolve that relationship-wrecking gristle, but Jehovah does: "Be kind to one another, tenderhearted, forgiving one another, even as God in Christ forgave you" (Ephesians 4:32 NKJV).

Let's discuss the heart-gristle eradicators in this New Testament passage a little more in depth.

* *Be kind to one another.* "Yeah, right. You must not understand my life, Lord. I'm supposed to be kind even when my lazy neighbor sees me struggling to get the kids and melting groceries out of the car and coldly returns to reading her book?"

Yep. Even then. Hard to digest, I know, but Papa God will deal with her in His time and on His terms (see the scripture at the beginning of this chapter). In the meantime, our kindness is not dependent on anyone else's behavior. Christ-followers don't wait for someone to be kind to us; we show them how it's done.

Kindness is similar to forgiveness in that we don't necessarily have to like someone to be kind to them.

Writer Samuel Johnson said, "Kindness is in our power, even when fondness is not."

Kindness and giving are soul sisters—you'll rarely find one without the other. Giving is the calloused hand of work on someone else's behalf. Kindness often wears a velvet glove. Neither draws attention to itself, but both respond as strong, capable fingers reaching out to offer help when help is needed. But we can only notice that help is needed when we're not completely engrossed by our own needs.

* *Be tenderhearted.* Heart tenderness is the willingness to enter someone else's world and share in their suffering; it's the step beyond kindness, usually motivated by compassion. But not always. Sometimes we got nothin'. We're emotionally bankrupt. Papa gets that, yet He can begin the heart-tenderizing process even if we simply show up with just a teaspoon of willingness.

* *Forgive one another.* Forgiveness is the element essential to finding inner peace. Resentment is poisonous; the poison gradually spreads and chokes out the life spark within you.

Forgiveness isn't about changing someone else; you don't have the power to do that. It's about changing something within you. It's about unlatching the hurt you wear like a heavy, bulletproof vest and dropping it to the floor so you can feel Papa God's warm, beating heart as He embraces you. He forgives you for your wrongs and wants you to do the same for those who wrong you.

Secondhand forgiveness may be even tougher.

Like secondhand smoke afflicts innocent bystanders, secondhand forgiveness is necessary when somebody hurts someone you love. The injured person may eventually forgive the offender, but you continue to harbor resentment indefinitely on your friend's behalf. And like cigarette smoke, unforgiveness pollutes and corrodes you internally.

Secondhand forgiveness is especially hard for us mama bears when somebody messes with our cubs. Our protective instincts kick into overdrive. But let's be a grown-up and take steps to end the lingering grudge when we hang on to it long after Junior has gotten over that nasty kid swiping his water pistol.

C'mon, Mama, you know the bitterness you're harboring. . . . Really. Let. It. Go.

It has been said that those who have been forgiven much, love much. "Bear with each other and forgive whatever grievances you may have against one another. Forgive as the Lord forgave you" (Colossians 3:13 NIV).

To truly forgive others as the Lord forgives us, we must tap into our Savior's supernatural grace. He specializes in grace—He proved that at Calvary, when Jesus willingly paid the price for our sins and died in our place.

Whereas justice is getting what you deserve and mercy is *not* getting what you deserve, grace is getting what you *don't* deserve. Pardon for the guilty, blatantly unmerited, and totally undeserved. Pretty tough to dole out when your so-called friend Hellon Wheels stabs you repeatedly in the back.

But as believers, we need to give jerks the benefit of grace. There's always something going on beneath the surface of their lives that we can't see.

Sometimes it's hard to remember that how we *feel* has nothing to do with forgiveness. We forgive as an act of the will, because Papa God commands us to, not necessarily because we feel forgiving. If we wait until we feel like it, we'll be the loneliest right person around.

When I'm trying to caulk a deep relationship crack, what helps me is to flip the forgiveness coin and look at it from another her-spective. I certainly hope the folks I've hurt over the years won't define me by my bad behavior. I look back on some of my horrid insensitivities and wince. It's my heartfelt prayer that others won't hold the nasty things I've said, hurtful things I've done, or stupid oversights I've made against me for the rest of my life. I'm more than a list of my past mistakes. Jesus made sure of that.

The folks who've wronged me are no different. If I can begin to see them through a lens of grace, forgiveness becomes easier.

We all know plenty of EGR people: Extra Grace Required. You can name a half dozen right now—those difficult people who require you to hock up an extra helping of grace. They may even be relatives, perhaps the kind who wound with friendly fire (the military term for a soldier shot by someone in her own army) and leave the fallen behind.

I love the story about the wild monkey who jumped on the railroad tracks to rescue a fallen friend who'd been shocked unconscious by a live wire at a train station in Kanpur, India. Awed humans left their train seats to snap pictures of one monkey lifting the other's motionless body off the tracks, dipping her in a mud puddle in an attempt to rouse her, and then steadily working her over with hands and teeth until the fallen companion finally opened her eyes and began moving again.

Wow. On so many levels. If monkeys can show such care and compassion for a fallen friend, I believe there's hope for people.

And the fallen are all around us—the shredders and the shredded. Those we need to forgive and others whose forgiveness we need. But if we ignore these unresolved needs, there will continue to be a whole lot of tough, unyielding, emotion-blocking heart-gristle.

Karen Scalf Linamen, author of *Pillow Talk,* says, "Bruised or otherwise, your feelings are yours, they belong to you, and you can hang on to them for as long as you want. For the rest of your life if you want to."[1] But please, my friend, choose not to. They'll be like Ebenezer Scrooge's chains around your neck.

As tempting as it sometimes is, we mustn't shoot the emotionally wounded or walk away from the fallen. "If it is possible, as far as it depends on you, live at peace with everyone" (Romans 12:18 NIV). We need to get rid of the heart-gristle holding back our attempts to restore broken relationships. No more fence posts.

This, dearest, is where chocolate melts beautifully into relationship cracks. Never negate the *yum* factor in friendship reparation.

We all know the way to a woman's heart is through her Ghirardelli, right? A pan of luscious brownies is a terrific nice-maker ice-breaker. Or a mocha latte. Or a plate of irresistible Chocolate Crack (from my *Too Blessed to be Stressed Cookbook*).

The peace-keeping qualities of chocolate cannot be stressed enough. In fact, I can't imagine why Jesus left it out of the Beatitudes: Blessed are the chocolate-givers, for they shall obtain forgiveness.

Remember, when it comes to resolving conflict:

> The one who apologizes is the bravest.
> The one who accepts is the strongest.
> The one who bears chocolate is the wisest.
> The one who offers to embrace is the humblest.
> But both are ever after the most changed.

* * *

A mom forgives us all our faults, not to mention one or two we don't even have.
—ROBERT BRAULT

* * *

Navigating the 'Hood

1. Is your heart tender toward that person who treated you like pig muck? Or worse, treated your *kid* like pig muck? No? So your heart is calloused with gristle. What steps can you take to allow Papa God to penetrate that gristle and apply His signature heart tenderizer?

2. Mark Twain said, "Kindness is the language which the deaf can hear and the blind can see." Can you cite a time when you responded to an EGR person with kindness? Who are the EGR people in your life right now? Brainstorm ways you can extend a little extra

grace to each of them this week.

3. Which of the heart-gristle eradicators in Ephesians 4:32 are currently your strong suit? Which need a little more effort?

4. Do you currently see yourself as shredded or a shredder? Why? In what ways can you caulk any relationship cracks that need mending? (By all means, feel free to include Chocolate Crack in your answer—maybe I should call it Chocolate Caulk!)

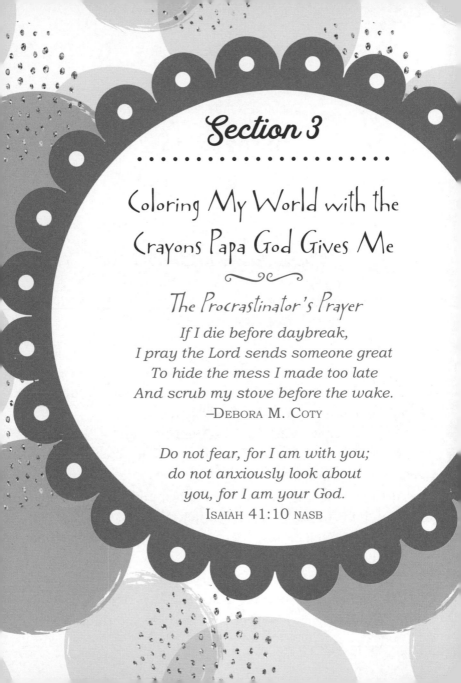

Section 3

· · · · · · · · · · · · · · · · · · · ·

Coloring My World with the Crayons Papa God Gives Me

The Procrastinator's Prayer

If I die before daybreak,
I pray the Lord sends someone great
To hide the mess I made too late
And scrub my stove before the wake.
–DEBORA M. COTY

Do not fear, for I am with you;
do not anxiously look about
you, for I am your God.
ISAIAH 41:10 NASB

CHAPTER 13

Detoxifying My Stinky Face

. . . .

Encouraging Others

Let the light of your face shine upon us, O Lord!
PSALM 4:6 NIV

*E*nlightenment strikes as my three-year-old grandbuddy Blaine watches me put on makeup:

Blaine: "What's that stuff do, Mimi?"

Me: "It's blush; it makes me look less dead, er, I mean it gives me more color."

Blaine: "Oh. Why do you want to be pink?"

Me: "I don't want to be pink. I just don't want to look like a walking marshmallow." [Silence while he contemplates this deep concept.]

Blaine: "What are you doing now, Mimi?"

Me: "Spraying perfume to make me smell pretty. See [holding out wrist for olfactory inspection]—what do you think?"

Blaine [making stinky face]: "Ugh. You smell like my Pull-Ups."

Sigh. Not exactly the demure elegance I was hoping to exude. But chuckling at Blaine-boy's stinky face made me realize something: many moms are unintentionally perfecting their stinky faces too.

Quite often when I pass the reflective surface of a mirror, microwave, or window, I'm floored at the toxic expression staring back at me. The thing is, I'm not necessarily angry. . .or sad. . .or even displeased. I'm just preoccupied. So preoccupied that I'm unaware of what my face is doing, and apparently when ignored, my facial muscles default to the same scowl I saw on my own mother's face countless times as a child.

I used to think she was always mad at me. And once when I asked her what I'd done, she seemed surprised and responded, "Why, nothing. I'm not upset with you; I'm focused on a million other things. Just ignore my face."

Impossible. No one can ignore your face. The face is the window into the mind, and we learn to read the expressions of others to discern what they're feeling. For example, a slack jaw, sagging muscles, and glazed-over eyes shout fatigue, boredom, and disinterest. How many times have our kids received this unspoken message while trying to give us a blow-by-blow report about the inchworm crossing the patio?

Frowns, pouts, and snarls obviously indicate indignation, resentment, and wrath (not unlike the mug of a perturbed bulldog), whereas a pleasant countenance and direct eye contact reflect interest, encouragement, and concern. A warm and sincere smile makes our kids feel accepted, uplifted, and loved from head to toe.

Oh, that we'd remember to employ this powerful self-esteem reinforcer every single day; what a difference we would make in our children's future selves.

Body language often speaks louder than words. Especially a mom's.

We *will* make parenting mistakes; there's no getting around that. It's part of the human package. But if we take every possible opportunity to communicate unconditional affection to our kids—and, when necessary, use words—they'll be better able to embrace Papa God's love too. "Above all, love each other deeply, because love covers over a multitude of sins" (1 Peter 4:8 NIV).

I'll always be grateful that even when I was a troublesome teenager (talk about a multitude of sins!), my mother demonstrated her unlimited love for me in countless unspoken ways. Although I never acknowledged it, I was acutely aware when she forfeited precious sleep to get up early to make my favorite breakfast.

And when she reached for the scrawny chicken wing on the platter at the dinner table, she'd smile as she passed me both meaty legs. It wasn't until I was in my twenties that I realized she preferred drumsticks too.

I remember all the times she would approach me from behind (because she knew I'd turn away if I saw her coming), wrap her arms around me, and quickly squeeze tender momsense into me. Although I remained as unresponsive as a statue, her whispered "I love you" registered deep within my rebellious spirit and I never doubted her devotion, regardless of how difficult I made her life.

These insightful words from a much wiser teen than me ring true: "The best thing parents can do is make sure their children know they're loved. They can make a lot of mistakes, but so long as their kids know they're loved, that's what matters."

There's comfort in knowing we don't have to be perfect parents to raise godly children, isn't there? Our God is used to working with imperfection. Matter of fact, He can work with anything, doesn't even have to be human. You know, in the Bible, Yahweh used a stubborn donkey (Numbers 22:27–31), a noisy bird (Matthew 26:74–75), and hungry swine (Luke 15:14–16) to accomplish His purposes.

Listen, if the Almighty can use an ass, a chicken, and a pig, He can surely use you and me! (I don't know about you, but I've been each one of those at least once today already.)

But we can stymie our own usefulness if we're not careful. Perpetual busyness can skew our best intentions and alter our motivation from "How can I serve others?" to "How can I get out of this?" Our focus shifts from helping someone else, or accomplishing something with eternal repercussions, to simply surviving another day. We depend on our own limited resources to limp along, instead of tapping into Papa God's unlimited power to glide.

Since we've already broached the subject of pigs, let me risk this analogy. Sorta like the Three Little Pigs, we become one of these Three Little Moms:

1. Straw Mom: Sees the task before her as overwhelming, a sure failure, or not worth her time, so she does the least possible to get by. She flies by the seat of her

pants, implementing many make-do shortcuts.

2. Stick Mom: Tries but is easily overwhelmed by stress. She starts then stops. Starts then stops again. Her exhausting efforts tend to crash to the ground with the least little breeze.

3. Brick Mom: Accepts the daunting challenge before her and approaches it brick by brick. She prayerfully establishes a solid plan and perseveres, holding on to the hope of accomplishment and depending on divine guidance along the way.

It's not too late to change your pig status, you know. The big, bad wolf has not yet come huffing. If you don't like being a Straw Mom, you can do something about it. To borrow a cliché, be the change you want to see. Your fam will see that change radiating from the inside out. They'll read it in your snout, er, countenance.

Yes, body language sends signals loud and clear about what's going on inside of us—maybe a little too blatantly sometimes. We can't disguise inattention. Even when we think we're hiding our preoccupation from the kiddos, we're not. Distraction is a mom's worst enemy; it sends destructive and worth-shattering messages we don't mean to relay.

Seriously, sister-mom—we're never *not* communicating. When we're glued to our phones, we're sending a distinct message to the child standing before us, craving our attention: "Someone else is more important to me than you."

And when we're torn away from our electronic devices by the urgency of kid-needs, what is our expression saying?

Although we may not be screaming (yet), does our demeanor betray the annoyance and frustration simmering within?

Think about your response to these convicting questions every mom should ask herself:

* Does my expression usually edify people—especially my children—or frighten the bejeebies out of them? What is my face projecting right now?

* Are the people around me—my personal mission field—being blessed, confused, or intimidated by my countenance today?

* Does the love of Jesus shine through my eyes and encourage through my smile?

* Has my face caught on to the joy of the Lord in my heart?

You already know that the words we use with our kiddos are crucial to their development. Who could ever forget how that simple truth is exemplified by the discerning maid Aibileen in *The Help*: "You is kind. You is smart. You is important." No wiser words of affirmation were ever uttered to a tiny human sponge soaking up the foundational ingredients for a lifetime of God-ordained self-worth.

Mother Teresa said, "Not all of us can do great things. But we can do small things with great love." It's not the big things we do that impact our children most; it's how present we are when *they* do things. That's a mom's biggest contribution to her child's development: her loving presence. Her attention. Her assurance that this little person is indeed important.

We don't want to miss experiencing the simple, everyday

discovery moments that shape our child's expanding worldview. Like the time a fascinated three-year-old was watching a neighbor nurse her new baby. "She's having milk for breakfast," Mom explained. After a moment of wide-eyed thought, the girl asked, "Is there orange juice in the other one?"

We all recognize that living in the mom-moment can be difficult to accomplish. To savor and enjoy the fleeting hours we have with our little buddy before he suddenly morphs into a big honkin' dude. To bedazzle our sweet little fairy princess with frills, bows, and lace before she pushes us away and crowns herself Drama Queen of the Universe.

So many real and pseudo-emergencies tug at our attention, causing even more disruption, derailment, and disorder—for example, those pesky breeding dishes (one of my Coty Near-Facts of Science). Yes, ma'am, you've seen it happen: dishes left in the sink reproduce overnight. Leave one small bowl soaking, and by morning there are three full place settings.

In the resonating words of ChannelMom.com blogger Amber Kanallakan:

> As I look at the state of my kitchen and the very unfinished to-do list on the fridge, I see important things that need to be dealt with. But when I let Jesus be my mentor for living in the present, I can look past the messy counter and see my three kids calling for my attention. Suddenly, I see that I have a choice: I can focus on the chaos and loudness of life, or I can look past the mess and navigate through the noise to really see and hear the true needs of the ones closest to me.[1]

Yes, we do have a choice in what kind of mom we are.

I choose to be a beautiful mom, even if my kids and I are the only ones looking. It's Papa God's smile that makes me beautiful, and I can smile His smile because I'm secure in Christ. Smiling promotes trust, reflects positivity, and helps others relax. It connects people. It makes me more approachable. Plus it's guaranteed to lift my own mood every time.

Hmm. Maybe I should tell my face the good news more often. Maybe I should make a serious effort to be more aware of my subconscious stinky face and offer my countenance to the Lord as an instrument of praise.

Just don't ask me to ditch the Eau de Pull-Ups.

· ·

Mom: the person who loves you unconditionally. Momster: what happens to Mom after she counts to three.
—A FORMER CHRONIC DOGHOUSE DWELLER

· ·

Navigating the 'Hood

1. Have you ever been shocked to discover a stinky face staring back at you from your microwave door? What was your reaction?

2. When is it hardest for you to stay focused on your kiddos? What are your biggest distractions? Do electronic devices tempt you away from living mom-moments with your family? How can you become more present?

3. Consider the lovely benediction found in Numbers 6:24–26 (NASB): "The LORD make His face shine on you, and be gracious to you; the LORD lift up His countenance on you, and give you peace." What do you think this scripture means? In what ways can the Lord lift up His countenance on you? How can it bring you peace?

4. So which of the three little pigs, er, I mean moms, are you: Straw Mom, Stick Mom, or Brick Mom? Which would you *like* to be? How can you get there from here?

CHAPTER 14

Zombie in Sweats

. . . .

Finding Elusive Rest

*It's useless to rise early and go to bed late, and work
your worried fingers to the bone. Don't you know he
[God] enjoys giving rest to those he loves?*
PSALM 127:2 MSG

*D*id you know that in Japan, people literally work
themselves to death? For many businesses, fourteen-
hour workdays are the norm and few take vacations, fearing
resentment from coworkers if they take days off in a culture that
values conformity and company loyalty. In fact, you're viewed
as a wimp if you use all your allotted vacay days; most people
are allowed an average of twenty per year but take only four.

Working overtime for free—sometimes up to one hundred
hours per month—is common among workers who feel
uncomfortable going home before their workaholic bosses. So
no one leaves.

The incidence of workers dropping dead of heart attack or cerebral hemorrhage rose so high that the government passed a law making employers legally responsible for their workers sticking to reasonable work hours and taking designated holidays.

Hey, sister-mom, can you imagine someone standing over you with a stopwatch droning, "Time to stop chasing kids now; that laundry can wait. Drop the fry pan. I demand that you sit down, put your feet up, and have a cup of hot tea."

Ah, what a slice of heaven that would be for every mom whose grumplitude soars off the charts because Toddler Timmy shimmies naked through the doggy door yet *again* to entertain the neighbors, while Kindergartner Katie sneaks the phone behind the couch and rings up a nice lady in Iceland.

Grumplitude? It's the scale of attitudinal grumpiness that fluctuates in direct relation to a woman's (a) blood sugar, (b) hormones, and (c) sleep tank. If your grumplitude gauge is flashing crimson, you'll know because evacuation proceedings of every living thing in your immediate vicinity will be fully operational. If they're not already hiding, they're running.

Becoming a grumplitude manager is the unspoken goal of every mom. Grumpiness is insidious and infectious. Who wants to exist in a perpetual fatigue-induced snit? Or hang around someone who is?

You think your grumpiness is justified because you're overworked? According to Guinness World Records, the greatest number of children born to one mother is sixty-nine. This woman, an eighteenth-century Russian peasant, had twenty-seven pregnancies, all multiples: sixteen pairs of twins, seven sets of triplets, and four sets of quads.

I'm betting her tombstone said, "Rest in Peace. Finally."

Multitasking has become a way of life for twenty-first-century moms as well. We may not have to milk cows, bake bread, and sew our fingers bloody, but we still mop till we drop, mother till we're smothered, and cram twenty-eight hours' worth of work into a twenty-four-hour day. Although all kinds of electronic gizmos have been designed to make our lives easier, techno-tasking has created its own brand of stress as the persistent pings, dings, and rings of those ever-present distraction devils *demand* our attention.

Everybody wants a piece of us. But Papa God wants some peace for us.

So where does a zombified 24-7 working mom turn for a smidge of tranquility?

Thankfully, you and I don't have to wait until we're laid in a grave for an extended dirt nap to find peace. Respite may be elusive, but it's not impossible.

You're rolling your eyeballs right now, aren't you? The last time your doctor asked how much sleep you were getting, you answered, "Well, when I sneeze, my eyes close." Okay, point taken. So far your motherhood experience has been "No rest for the weary," but as someone who's been there, done that, let me assure you there *is* something you can do when you suddenly realize one day you've become a zombie in sweats.

It's estimated that 50 percent of Americans have trouble falling asleep and/or staying asleep; about 15 percent struggle with chronic sleeplessness and rise in the morning exhausted.[1] When insomnia becomes chronic, lasting six months or longer, it can wreak serious physical, emotional, and social havoc, including depression.

Ever wonder why some mornings you have trouble remembering to check the breakfast milk for chunks? Sleep is essential to memory—your brain uses those "downtime" hours to maintain your memory storage and keep retrieval systems working efficiently. Without enough sleep, your poor brain can't catch up with all that filing; barrels of unprocessed information pile up all over the place, cluttering your mind, fatiguing your spirit, and leaving you irritable and cranky because you can't seem to remember squat.

Know what else? Lack of sleep creates hormone imbalances that make you crave higher-calorie foods. Ack! Frumpy, grumpy, *and* lumpy—who needs that?

Here are ten simple changes you can make to decom-stress sleep time and grab a few refreshing zzz's (thanks to Dr. Mehmet Oz for his contributions)[2]:

1. *Develop a routine.* Sleep in a designated spot at a designated time. Routine is important for tipping off your body that it's time to close up shop instead of building a new one.

2. *Unplug.* A 2017 Nielsen report revealed that adults ages eighteen to forty-nine spend an average of six to seven hours per week on social media.[3] No wonder we can't wind down. Ditch the electronic devices an hour before bedtime; not only does the relentless stimulation keep you wired up and fired up, but the glowing lights tend to suppress your brain's secretion of melatonin, the hormone that produces sleep.

3. *Work it, baby.* Studies show that regular exercise three to four times weekly, two or more hours before bedtime, definitely helps induce sleep. Walk, run, work out, swim, spin, kickbox, dance, play tennis, join the roller derby. . .get your heart rate up and your blood pressure down. Dreamland is your awesome reward.

4. *Pass the parchment.* Keep a pad and pen by your bedside to write down all those to-dos that pop into your head so you don't have to remember them. It's instant stress relief to turn off those brain circuits and turn over the job of recollection to the mighty pen.

5. *Stick a sock on it.* Researchers have found that wearing socks to bed keeps your feet warmer than your body, which promotes sleep. This works well for me unless it's July in Tampa, when I progressively strip all night long. By 4:00 a.m. I end up naked, spread-eagled on the bathroom tile floor.

6. *Feed the beast.* A light, healthy snack before bed (avoid caffeine!) is actually a good thing; it silences that nerve-grating stomach growl and squelches cravings for junk food by balancing appetite-regulating hormones. However, do limit liquids, due to the BBP (Bursting Bladder Phenomenon), another Coty Near-Fact of Science. The BBP is that inexplicable law of nature that expands one six-ounce cup of hot tea consumed before bedtime into two quarts an hour after you hit the sack. And then mysteriously dredges up another quart every half hour thereafter. It's the gift that keeps on giving. . .all night long.

7. *Evict nasty bedfellows.* This one's yucko but important. If persistent allergy symptoms keep you awake, consider investing in a new mattress. Dust and—are you sitting down?—dust *mites* sometimes gather in nooks and crannies of mattresses older than five years and can trigger annoying allergic reactions. *Shudder.* 'Nuff said.

8. *Melt away stress.* A steamy shower or warm bubble bath just before bed (along with your favorite soft, nonstimulating music) will work relaxation wonders. I should know; my hot bath at two o'clock this morning did the trick.

9. *Cuddle something.* After you've poured out consolation and reassurance to little people all day, being on the receiving end of physical affirmation can refill your own emotional teapot. If available, a husband is a delightful source of soothing touch, as long as he understands that *sleep* is the end goal here. A special plush animal or soft blanket can also help calm frazzled nerves (yes, adults can have binkies too!).

10. *Marinate in God's Word.* "In peace I will lie down and sleep, for you alone, LORD, make me dwell in safety" (Psalm 4:8 NIV). Reflecting on a favorite Bible passage is a wonderful way to bring peace and relaxation to your soul. One of my midnight go-tos is Matthew 11:28–29 (NIV): "Come to me, all you who are weary and burdened, and I will give you rest. Take my yoke upon you and learn from me, for I am gentle and humble in heart, and you will find rest for your souls."

Dearest mom-friend, if all else fails, remember that you're not alone—mothers have functioned in the same sleep-deprived state for thousands of years and have not only survived but lived productive lives honoring our Creator. We're a sisterhood of slightly sagging spiritual warriors. But, as Papa God reminds us, "My grace is sufficient for you, for my power is made perfect in weakness" (2 Corinthians 12:9 NIV).

And what weaker vessel to perfect His power than a zombie mombie?

• •

Mombie: a sleep-deprived mother surviving on caffeine, drooly kisses, and toothless smiles.
—A MOMBIE INEXPLICABLY WILLING TO DO IT ALL OVER AGAIN

• •

Navigating the 'Hood

1. What tends to send your grumplitude meter soaring off the charts?

2. How many hours of sleep per night do you need? How many do you average? Would you like to work on improving that?

3. When would you describe yourself as a zombie in sweats? What time of day do you feel most like the underbelly of a slug?

4. Which of the ten sleep-time decom-stressors in this chapter will you begin to implement this week? Next week?

CHAPTER 15

Mommas in the Trenches

· ·

Mom-Courage

You were tired out by the length of your road,
yet you did not say, "It is hopeless." You found
renewed strength, therefore you did not faint.
ISAIAH 57:10 NASB

∽‿ℚℭ‿∽

*B*eing a mom is *hard.* In fact, the very nature of mothering—of conceiving, carrying, then birthing a tiny, ever-hungry, screaming, pooping, attention-craving human—involves hardship. Loving that squalling little person, meeting his needs, and fostering healthy development all come prepackaged with unforeseen difficulties.

Meeting these maternal challenges head-on brings out tremendous courage in many women; one is my friend Evelyn Mann.

Evelyn's pregnancy started out with great joy; she and her

husband Ralph were thrilled to be expecting their firstborn. But at the twenty-week ultrasound, they were informed that their son was "not developing normally."

Spirit-crumbling words for any momma.

Further nerve-wracking tests revealed that the baby (Samuel, they called him) had a rare and fatal form of dwarfism. Fatal. As in *he won't live more than one day after birth.* Abortion was recommended. There were only two known cases of children with this condition who had made it past infancy—*ever.* One died at age three, the other at seven.

Evelyn was told there was no prayer of her little boy ever growing, learning, or moving on his own. Zero. But you know what? There's *always* a prayer.

In this horrendous situation in which they were offered absolutely no natural hope, Evelyn and Ralph found supernatural hope. Peace in the midst of chaos blanketed them as they clung to the biblical promise that whatever happened with Samuel, "the peace of God, which transcends all understanding, will guard your hearts and your minds in Christ Jesus" (Philippians 4:7 NIV).

They chose not to abort, but to love baby Samuel to the best of their ability for every brief minute he shared with them on this earth.

Today, over a decade later, Samuel is their little miracle Mann! He's an adorable imp with a contagious, playful smile. Not only is he learning and growing, but he gleefully pops Cheerios into his mouth and zips around on a customized scooter (allow Samuel to bring a smile to your face at miraclemann.com). He's the delight of his parents' lives and has impacted countless thousands (including me) with his incorrigible zest for life.

It has become Evelyn's burning desire to offer encouragement to other families facing "hopeless" situations, to demonstrate by one family's courage that even a negative diagnosis is not beyond God's reach.

Mom-courage is not something women manufacture out of the clear blue sky; it's the byproduct of fierce, relentless love and is possible, in its truest form, only through a transfusion of Papa God's supernatural strength. The strength that flows unimpeded when our own has ebbed into a stagnant puddle. The strength that keeps us running the everyday marathon when we're sure we cannot possibly take one more step.

Supernatural is what fills the void when you let go of the natural.

"Be strong with the Lord's mighty power" (Ephesians 6:10 NKJV). His *mighty power*. That's the secret ingredient that makes some women excel as mothers and others. . .well, not so much.

Let's look at some biblical examples of both good and not-so-good mothers.

Good Bible Mothers

❋ *Mary, mother of Jesus (Luke 2:19).* Mary taught all of us moms by example that when we're awed or bewildered or emotionally overcome by the miracle of our precious child (if you're like me, this happens often), we should pause to treasure the moment, tucking it away in our hearts and pondering it often. Mary is our role model of a supportive mom: protective, prayerful, present. She was her child's biggest cheerleader; Mary lived her life as a disciple of her own son, the Savior of the world (Acts 1:14). Girls, we have big sandals to fill.

* *Deborah (Judges 4–5).* Deborah was a brave working mother who was a trailblazer in a time when women were not promoted; she proved that women could do anything men could do (and sometimes better!). Deb was a respected judge, prophet, military advisor, and political leader to whom her country's highest army general deferred. In fact, the dude refused to go to battle unless Deborah went with him (Judges 4:8). Deb's courage and willingness to do anything Yahweh Tsuri ("The Lord Is My Rock"—don't you love all the Hebrew names for God?) called her to do saved her country from annihilation.

* *Sarah (Genesis 21:6, 22:2).* Isaac's mother chose to lean on trust: First that Elohim ("Mighty Creator") would provide her long-awaited child as He'd promised (although she had to wait till she was ninety to trade her wheelchair for a baby stroller and prune juice lattes for apple juice sippy cups). And trust yet again that her husband Abraham accurately heard the Most Sovereign God instruct him to sacrifice the happy boy she loved more than life itself (I'm afraid my trust would have wavered big-time on that one). Despite her shattered heart, Sarah courageously allowed Abraham to lead their son away to his death. Her stalwart faith was rewarded when Yahweh Shalom ("The Lord Is Peace") spared Isaac and made Sarah and Abe the parents of countless descendants and nations.

✳ *Naomi (Ruth 1:6–13).* When calamity struck, Naomi refused to wither away. Instead, she rose up, made hard decisions, and began a long journey with her one remaining dependent, her widowed daughter-in-law Ruth. When Naomi landed back in Bethlehem, she forged out a new normal and assumed leadership of her unconventional family (perhaps something like you've courageously done, dear single mom?). Naomi became a clever matchmaker for Ruth and her hot crush Boaz (Ruth 3:1–5), who, after connecting against all odds, became the ancestors of King David and eventually Jesus.

✳ *Hannah (1 Samuel 1:6–8).* Hannah kept hoping and praying, despite chronic despair over infertility, a nasty wife-in-law (her husband's cocky other wife), and her spouse's sincere insensitivity as exemplified in verse 8 (NASB): "Then Elkanah her husband said to her, 'Hannah, why do you weep and why do you not eat and why is your heart sad? Am I not better to you than ten sons?'" (Typical male response—he wants to help but doesn't really understand the problem.) Through years of depression, Hannah kept praying (1:10), becoming a role model of perseverance despite trying circumstances. When El Olam ("The Everlasting God") granted her heart's desire and she became pregnant, Hannah honored her promise to give her child back to the Lord (her son became the mighty prophet Samuel) and she was blessed with five more children (2:21). Hannah always— *always*—remembered to give praise and thanks to the Giver of her blessings.

* *Harlot in King Solomon's court (1 Kings 3:16–27).* This demoralized single woman (during a time when unwed pregnancy was often a death sentence) was bravely willing to give up her newborn to another woman (adoption) rather than kill him. Not unlike the dilemma many women face today when considering abortion in the event of an unplanned pregnancy.

* *Widow of Zarephath (1 Kings 17:10–24).* This woman sacrificially gave her last bite of food to her hungry son. Later when the boy grew ill and died, she gathered her chutzpah and boldly approached the prophet Elijah, asking for a miracle from Jehovah Shammah ("The Lord Is There"). She got one; because of her faith, tenacity, and mom-courage, her son was raised from the dead.

* *Prophet's widow (2 Kings 4:1–7).* When creditors came to enslave her two sons to pay off her dead husband's debt, she trusted that Adonai (God) could—and would—help her. She bravely sought out the prophet Elisha and received a bottomless jar of valuable oil as her money-providing miracle.

* *Shunammite woman (2 Kings 4:8–37).* When this generous, infertile woman provided food and lodging to Elisha, he interceded with the Almighty on her behalf and a son was born to her and her husband. When the boy was later struck with a lethal headache and died in his mother's lap, she didn't panic, but saddled her donkey and galloped away to find Elisha, whose side she refused to leave (verse 30) until he petitioned the Great I Am (God) to restore her child. Her calm

assurance, stubborn faith, and dogged determination saved her boy.

Not-So-Good Bible Mothers

✳ *Hagar (Genesis 21:9–21).* Hagar was the mother of Abraham's son Ishmael and the maid of his wife Sarah. Hagar was a haughty-spirited bully who taunted Sarah's infertility (Genesis 16:4). After Sarah got fed up with Hagar's insolence and sent her away, Hagar threw her hands in the air and gave up when things got tough. She simply quit trying to survive and plopped herself down in the desert to watch her child die. But Yahweh (God) mercifully came to their rescue, providing water, food, and shelter.

✳ *Rebekah (Genesis 25:28; 27:5–46; 28:1–5).* Rebekah loved one of her two children—twins, no less—more than the other. After eavesdropping on a conversation not meant for her, she hatched a devious plot to help her pride and joy (Jacob) betray his father, her own husband (Isaac). She later sneakily coerced her husband again on Jacob's behalf, manipulating Isaac to do things her way when it came to finding Jacob a wife. I consider conniving, deceitful, self-serving Rebekah the queen mother of dysfunctional families.

✳ *Mrs. Zebedee (Matthew 20:20–24).* She was the mother of Jesus' disciples James and John, who were known as "sons of thunder." I've often wondered if "thunder" referred to their explosive ma. Mrs. Z was so nearsighted in her quest to usher her boys to head-of-the-class that when Jesus had barely finished anguishing his heart out over his approaching death (20:18–19), she—insensitively and inappropriately—butted in with her own selfish agenda. Thunder-Ma brazenly demanded, in front of God and all the saints, that her two sons be proclaimed second and third in command in Jesus' upcoming kingdom. Not one to let ignorance get in her way (she totally misunderstood the nature of Jesus' kingdom), Mrs. Z barreled ahead, stomping on toes aplenty and sowing discord among friends. Diplomacy be hanged, Thunder-Ma was all about self-promoting her own.

I'd like to think I haven't developed a reputation like Thunder-Ma, but I do recall a few instances when I might have earned the title. Provoked, I can quickly become the Chihuahua facing down a hungry bear in my author-friend Shellie Rushing Tomlinson's hilarious blog story about a thunderous little dog bravely encountering the gargantuan foe. The wee warrior stood firm, barking her teensy lungs out, but steadily lost ground against the bear, which evidently had a craving for Mexican food. In the nick of time, the purse dog's owner swooped to the rescue, slugging the surprised bear upside his snarling snout.

Wildlife officials sagely commented, "All's well that ends well, but we do not recommend punching a bear in the face."[1]

I think Jesus might similarly say to us little Chi-mamas fighting in the trenches, "I love when you're courageous, but I'd rather you let Me wear the boxing gloves."

A father may turn his back on his child, brothers
and sisters may become inveterate enemies,
husbands may desert their wives, wives their husbands.
But a mother's love endures through all.
—WASHINGTON IRVING

Navigating the 'Hood

1. When, during your motherhood journey, have you
   depended on Papa God's courage when you hadn't
   enough of your own? What was the outcome? Would
   you say you *need* supernatural strength to keep your
   mom-courage well stocked?

2. Which of the examples of good and not-so-good biblical
   mothers do you identify with most? Why? Any specific
   qualities speak to you?

3. Are there times when you could be awarded the
   title "Thunder-Ma"? What makes your thunder roll
   and lightning strike? Consider how you might apply
   2 Chronicles 32:8 (NIV): "With us is the LORD our God
   to help us and to fight our battles."

4. Now consider this from Psalm 27:14 (NKJV): "Wait on the
   LORD; be of good courage, and He shall strengthen your
   heart." What is the Lord saying to you in this passage
   regarding a specific circumstance in your life right now?

CHAPTER 16

My Hair Stylist Is from Oz

· ·

Confidence

Am I now trying to win the approval of men, or of God?
GALATIANS 1:10 NIV

∼ ✑ ∽

*D*o you ever catch a glimpse of your grodiest mom-self in
a mirror and wonder, *What in the world happened to the
nattily dressed, beautifully manicured, meticulously made-up,
hair-cut-and-styled, attractive me I used to be?* The time and
attention necessary to maintain that trendy persona somehow
slip-slid away between ditching dirty diapers and scraping
dried oatmeal off table legs.

And then your self-respect slip-slid close behind. *Ick.*

Most days you feel like your ragged self is a graffiti-plastered
cement wall in a run-down section of town. You do your best
to spray-paint over the imperfections, but it only changes the
color. There's no escaping that battered, droopy, hideous wall
beneath.

Like that broken wall, broken self-esteem permeates every aspect of our lives.

I once heard acclaimed military biographer Carlo D'Este discuss his book on the life of General George Patton, *Patton: A Genius for War.* D'Este's well-researched book disclosed the little-known fact that General Patton was dyslexic, and his driving ambition to excel despite this rather substantial weak spot was the compelling force behind his incredible military career.

Patton's famous tough exterior was really a veneer concealing his lifelong battle with poor self-esteem.

After the book released, D'Este was approached by numerous dyslexics who gratefully adopted Patton as their role model; D'Este's book had given them new confidence. At one bookstore signing, a six-foot-five-inch T-Rex of a man hung back shyly; after the line dwindled, he approached D'Este. "I really liked your book. But the thing is, I can't read." He admitted that his wife read the book to him, and he'd never in his life felt less demoralized by his secret shame and more energized to succeed despite it.

Sister-mom, we are like Patton: flawed generals fighting our own daily battles.

Faults-R-Us, girlfriend. Daylong bedhead, grape-jelly–stained tees, shaggy unibrows, jiggling thigh-u-lite, leg fur, sleep-deprived raccoon eyes, fingernails that look like you dug out of Alcatraz. . .all part of the mom download. The energies that once carefully accentuated our positives are now channeled elsewhere. Some might even say having kids is a liability to looking and feeling our best.

But the difference between "ability" and "liability" is a lie.

Our assets and abilities are still there—they're just lying low for a while.

I'll never forget the day my four-year-old burst into the bathroom just as I was exiting the shower (honestly, is *nothing* sacred?). Unabashed, he watched me scurry across the room to grab a towel. "Mom," he said earnestly, "why does your heinie keep moving after you stop?"

Mama mia, that's the kind of negative self-talk we don't want—our thighs whispering together behind closed drawers as we walk. But scarfing leftover PB&J scraps, hot dog belly buttons (what my kids used to call hot dog ends), and drool-sodden cookies piles up undisclosed calories and we can end up with mom-creep. You know, a pound here and a pound there, creeping in to expand hard-body prebaby figures into DC-10s.

Hey, in my humble but accurate opinion, the current consume-fewer-calories-than-you burn-to-lose-weight system would benefit from an updated clause. Based on common banking principles, I'm proposing that heaven institute a calorie bank in which everyone would have their own account.

Yep—a calorie account to count calories. A fat deposit box, if you will.

Here's how it works: Say I am presented with a triple-chocolate brownie that triggers my salivary glands to burst into geysers. I am nearly drowning in my own secretions, courageously attempting to withstand temptation. Despite the rich chocolaty goodness screaming my name, I heroically take only one bite instead of downing the whole wretched thing.

Not only should the calories of that gutsy, self-controlled

bite *not* count, I should get resistance bonus points deposited in the calorie bank—a credit to my account to be used at my later discretion. Or indiscretion.

Say my neighbor brings over a whopping slice of her famous scrumpdillyicious Death by Chocolate Cheesecake and stands there on my doorstep, smiling her neighborliest as she hands me a fork, waiting for me to dive right in.

Now I ask you, what's the Christian thing to do?

It would be inexcusable to hurt her feelings. Nor would I have to with the new calorie banking system. I simply withdraw a few (hundred) of those bonus points from my fat deposit box and—voilà—my account is balanced. No weight is gained. No pants require unbuttoning. Everyone's happy.

Sure beats the weight management system my fellow writer Janette Barber uses. Janette claims, "When I buy cookies I eat just four and throw the rest away. Bur first I spray them with Raid so I won't dig them out of the garbage later. Be careful, though, because Raid really doesn't taste that bad."

Speaking of cookies and desperation, did you hear about the Florida woman who was arrested for whacking her roommate over the head with a board for stealing her Thin Mints? Seriously. Can you believe people would go to jail over Thin Mints? Now Samoas, sure. . .

But I do believe there's a link between chocolate and longevity. I read about one dear grandma who, on her 105th birthday, told the local newspaper that she credited Cadbury chocolate before bed every night with helping her live so long. For her 106th birthday, Cadbury sent her 106 pounds of chocolate. Kudos, Cadbury! (My personal pièce de résistance is Cadbury milk chocolate with almonds.)

Like the plaque in my kitchen says, "Chocolate is God's apology for broccoli." Plus it's a top-notch stress reliever.

My choco-friend Mo (Morgynne Northe MacDougall) has a theory: "Stress causes the female body to think it's in crisis, so it retains fat to deal with the crisis. Eating M&M's releases endorphins that help reduce stress and promote a sense of well-being. Therefore, M&M's actually reduce the potential for weight gain during times of stress."

Hey, I'll bite. Definitely my kind of logic.

Okay, back to the focus of this chapter: confidence. Sagging self-esteem isn't just about appearance, is it? It's a nagging, underlying fear that we're not competent to fulfill our mom-role. That we're not doing it right. That we're screwing up our kids for life and inadvertently producing a generation of sociopaths.

Why do so many of us feel inadequate? I suspect it has to do with self-comparison. We hold our worst selves up—on our most chaotic, nonproductive, messy, psycho-kid days—next to the most perfect mom we know; and, of course, we fall short. Subsequently, we feel like a disgraceful fake—a total failure in carrying out basic mothering requirements.

But we must resist the temptation to compare our middle to someone else's ending. Her current struggle is in a different place, probably a place you can't see. Maybe organization isn't her weakness; teaching her son kindness is. She might have sparkling grout and a kid who rips the legs off grasshoppers.

You're an apple; she's a persimmon. No comparison. Your strengths are in different areas. You're working on different challenges.

Hear this now: according to Romans 8:39 (NIV), "Neither height nor depth, nor anything else in all creation, will be able to separate us from the love of God that is in Christ Jesus our Lord." In other words, Papa God is saying, "I love you and there's nothing you can do about it. You're not someone who needs to be fixed; you are enough just as you are. You, My daughter, are a unique gift from Me to the world."

Did you catch that? He *knows* you're human and you sometimes screw up. He created you! And He created you to be at your best when you depend on Him: "Forget about self-confidence; it's useless. Cultivate God-confidence" (1 Corinthians 10:12 MSG). We don't need to be hamstrung by low self-esteem. If we live for Christ and embrace His unconditional acceptance, we'll bask in Christ-esteem, regardless of our shortcomings.

And that should give us utmost confidence.

In the wise words of writer Peter T. McIntyre, "Confidence comes not from always being right, but from not fearing to be wrong."[1] It's okay to flub up sometimes. If we're leaning on God's Word and prayerfully making the best decisions we can for our families, Papa God will bless our mess.

Regardless of what anyone in a skin suit thinks.

So you don't have to obsess about others evaluating your mom-performance. They probably will; such is human nature. So what? Their opinions amount to spit. Someone else's opinion of you doesn't have to become your reality. No one can judge you but Papa God, and He's not condemning you. He's sympathetically hearing your cries, tenderly treasuring your tears, and graciously forgiving your mistakes.

He's standing by to fill you—if you ask—with His unfailing

power and give you a fresh start. "But we have this treasure [faith in Jesus Christ] in jars of clay [human bodies] to show that this all-surpassing power is from God and not from us. We are hard pressed on every side, but not crushed; perplexed, but not in despair; persecuted, but not abandoned; struck down, but not destroyed" (2 Corinthians 4:7–9 NIV).

Wow—"hard pressed on every side. . .perplexed. . .struck down"—is that a good description of a mom's average day, or what?

I love what Ruth Bell Graham, wife of Billy Graham and mom of five, said about mothering, "If I cannot give [my children] a perfect mother, I can at least give them more of the one they've got. . . . I will take time to listen, time to play. Time to counsel and encourage. In a world of confusion and uncertainties, I will give them the eternal verities of the Word of God."[2] It's not our being perfect (*yeesh*—such an unrealistic expectation!) but rather our inching closer to Papa God today than we were yesterday that makes Him proud of us! Physically, spiritually, and emotionally, it's a triathlon, not a sprint.

In chef-speak, motherhood is a soufflé, not instant rice.

Just look at Papa's mode of operation for our long-term survival. Yahweh gave the wandering Israelites manna in the desert (Exodus 16) to survive. . .but only when they *really* needed it, and only enough for one day. He does the same for moms—manna strength when you need it most and just enough to get you through today. The good news is that He'll do the same tomorrow. And each day after that. One day at a time.

So, my dear girl, believe it because it's true: bedhead, unibrow, inadequacies and all—you are perfect to do the job Papa created you for. To think otherwise would be mommalpractice.

• •

One day I'll be thankful that my kid is strong willed,
but that will not be today. Not in this grocery store.
—MEME SMACK

• •

Navigating the 'Hood

1. Like General Patton, have you carefully constructed a veneer to conceal some secret imperfection? Do you think that "perfect" mom you know might have done the same? How can self-protective appearances be deceiving?

2. Listen to what Romans 8:1 (NLT) says to you about your mothering flaws: "There is no condemnation for those who belong to Christ Jesus."

3. Do you ever compare yourself to other mothers? In which ways do you feel you don't measure up? How can you adjust your way of thinking so that you don't feel so unfairly judged?

4. Name some specific ways Yahweh has provided mom-manna strength for you—just the right amount of help when you needed it most. Based on these past experiences, what can you expect for the future. . .and for today?

CHAPTER 17

Ripening Isn't Just for Bananas

· ·

Everyday Miracles

Listen for GOD's voice in everything you do,
everywhere you go.
PROVERBS 3:6 MSG

*J*n 1989, when Kellie Knapp was an eleven-year-old child of Christian medical missionaries in Somalia, civil war erupted. The mission compound housing her family was overrun by Muslim extremists, intent on ransacking the buildings and executing all missionaries.

The day of the surprise attack, Kellie's family barely had enough time to hide in a bedroom of their small cement house; Kellie curled up beneath a dresser while her mother, brother, and baby sister hid under the bed. Kellie's dad braced himself against the closed door. They could do nothing but wait, remain stone still, and pray desperately.

The tension was palpable, the stakes incredibly high. These invaders were known for dragging their victims out to the street, where they tortured and brutally killed them as an example to their other "enemies."

Kellie began praying for a quick death so she wouldn't have to watch her family die.

They heard pounding at their gate. With a crash, it was broken down. The terrifying sounds of running feet, staccato gunfire, and angry yelling reverberated as the band of terrorists searched for the family, waving machine guns and peering through screened windows and a glass door into the very room they were in.

Kellie's family could clearly see the militants, but the militants somehow couldn't see them. Almighty God had hidden them in plain view.

Three different groups of assailants ransacked the house that day, but not one person entered that bedroom. *Not one.* Their eyes were miraculously blinded to the presence of Kellie and her family.[1]

Whoa. Every time I read that story, I sprout fresh God-bumps.

Miracles. As new believers, we're amazed by the awe-inspiring biblical accounts of Jesus healing the sick, transforming hearts, even raising the dead. We know the Bible is bursting with 'em, but here's the soul-searing question: Do miracles still happen today?

Like Kellie, I wholeheartedly, absolutely, unequivocally shout *yes!*

That's because I've experienced them myself. And so have you, although perhaps you didn't recognize it at the time. It takes a certain amount of cultivated discernment and wide-open spiritual eyes to see the Lord's subtle (or even blatant!) intervention in a situation.

As we mature in our faith and spend more and more time in the presence of Papa God, we learn to recognize His style, His methods, His MO. Although you certainly can't put God in a box, and He does seem to love surprises, we'll better recognize His unique touch the longer we walk with Him. Our discernment of His interwoven involvement in our life ripens, and we're more aware of the everyday miracles through which He lavishes His love on us.

Sometimes miracles come out of the blue—unsolicited, unexpected, and practically unbelievable. (Lord, help our lame disbelief!)

Other times we develop calloused camel knees praying long and hard about a specific problem before Yahweh's answer presents itself.

Still other times, we find ourselves—like the Old Testament children of Israel fleeing Egyptian slavery (Exodus 12–14)—in a Red Sea moment, stuck between a hostile army on one side and a raging ocean of problems on the other. No good options; our choices are all lose-lose. We're doomed without supernatural intervention.

Then. . .He miraculously does. He intervenes without fanfare, usually with no resounding trumpets or booming timpani underscoring His covert movement. So subtle we'll miss the underlying source if we're not tuned in.

Because of our inexperience with divine intervention in our sequestered little worlds, we don't always recognize His everyday miracles for what they are. We chalk them up to luck, happenstance, or karma. C. S. Lewis said, "Miracles are a retelling in small letters of the very same story which is written across the whole world in letters too large for some of us to see."

Grace notes—that's what I call these special little touches from Papa God—serve to remind you that the details of your life are important to Him. That He's always watching. That He's got your back.

The trouble is that we get so wrapped up in the bustling busyness of mothering, we may not hear the grace notes. Their sweet consonance just floats right past our spiritual ears and out the bathroom window. But we *need* to hear those grace notes, sister, so we can twirl and dance and boogie down to the internal music with which our Creator underscores our lives. "God rewrote the text of my life when I opened the book of my heart to his eyes" (Psalm 18:24 MSG).

One of our memorable family grace notes occurred when six-year-old Matthew dropped a glass bottle in the garage. When it burst on the cement floor, glass shards took a hunk out of his lower leg. Chuck and I had a hard time stopping the bleeding and debated taking him to the ER, but it was getting late and he had to be up for school early the next morning, so we made the dubious decision to stabilize it ourselves.

By the time Matthew fell asleep, red streaks were beginning to run up his leg from the gaping, oozing wound.

In worried-mother mode, I tiptoed into his room with a flashlight and checked it every hour. For the first four hours, those red streaks inched upward. At 1:00 a.m., I prayed over

Matthew's sleeping body, laying my hands on his leg, petitioning earnestly for divine intervention.

At the 3:00 a.m. check, I couldn't believe my eyes! Not only were the scary red streaks completely gone, but the open wound had generated healthy new tissue at incredible speed, well on its way to closing up completely. He was truly being healed!

The next morning, Matthew stumbled into the kitchen groggy with sleep. He suddenly remembered his boo-boo and yanked up the leg of his jammies, where the only evidence of the accident was a thin red scar. "Wait—where did it go?" he asked, mystified. "Did I dream that I cut my leg, or did it really happen?"

The power of a praying mother. Never doubt it, sister-mom. I believe our Creator's hearing is specially attuned to the anguished cries of a mother for her own stake of creation, her precious child. Just as His heart broke over the suffering of His beloved Son, Jesus, He feels your exquisite pain when your child is in trouble.

An illegal driver with a DUI history slammed into the car of my bestie Jan and her husband on their way home from the hospital with their newborn son. Although infant car seats weren't required by law in 1982, Jan had felt strongly led to strap Jeremy in a car seat, which the responding EMS medic credited with saving his life. Jan sustained multiple facial lacerations and a broken jaw, but baby Jeremy slept through the whole ordeal.

In an ultra-cool God-twist, more than twenty years later, the same medic who worked that wreck "coincidentally" spoke at Jeremy's own paramedic school graduation. To complete the full circle, paramedic Jeremy happened to be called to the scene of a stabbing, where he labored to save the very same man who'd randomly smashed into his parents' car decades before.

Coincidentally. . .happened to. . .randomly. Hmm. Are these words that we casually use regarding our life circumstances without giving them due thought? Perhaps we should think about them. By giving "chance" credit for the miracles in our life, we're robbing Jehovah Jireh ("God Provides") of full credit for His amazing customized grace notes.

And we're not just talking about life-and-death situations here. Papa God specializes in everyday mini miracles. (Although calling a miracle "mini" is like saying you're a "little bit" pregnant!)

My friend Kim's teenage daughter, Lyann, got her class schedule the week before school started but noticed they had her in a class she'd already completed. Her dad went down to Student Affairs and explained the error; he was assured by a counselor that everything would be worked out before school started.

It wasn't. So concerned mom Kim started praying about it.

The second day of school, Lyann was told that the guidance counselors were overwhelmed so she'd have to wait. The third day she was informed they were handling schedule changes at lunch. So she got in line at lunch only to hear, "We're just working with juniors today."

The fourth day, when Lyann finally got to tell a counselor which class she wanted, the woman replied, "You're lucky you came when you did. The girl in line before you just dropped that class, so now there's an opening."

Lucky? Nah.

Papa God's track record proves otherwise.

• •

A baby is something you carry inside you for
nine months, in your arms for three years,
and in your heart until the day you die.
—MARY MASON

• •

Navigating the 'Hood

1. Is there a true-life miracle that gives you God-bumps like Kellie's story does for me?

2. Did you know that James, author of the New Testament epistle, acquired the nickname "Old Camel Knees" because of all the hours he spent on his knees in prayer? (Recorded in AD 325 by Eusebius of Caesarea in an account of church history.) What aspect of motherhood drives you to your knees, dear friend?

3. What Red Sea moment have you experienced? How did Papa God intervene? How did you recognize His fingerprints in the situation?

4. Can you think of a recent grace note (everyday miracle) in your own life? If you're having trouble answering that question, will you commit with me now to open your spiritual eyes wide and actively look for the subtle fingerprints of Papa in your everyday circumstances? Trust me, girlfriend—they're there.

CHAPTER 18

Gratitude Is Glade for the Soul

. . . .

Developing a Thankful Lifestyle

Give thanks in all circumstances; for this
is God's will for you in Christ Jesus.
1 THESSALONIANS 5:18 NIV

My friend Linda thanks God for her three-loads-per-day mound of laundry. Why? Because it means her four kids have towels, bedsheets, and clothes. She also pauses to give thanks before tackling each pile of dirty dishes in her sink because they're the result of having food to put on the table for her family.

Is Linda some kind of divergent supermom? Nah. She's just as exhausted as you at the end of the day; her gratitude for thankless, repetitive chores doesn't come naturally any more than yours does. But she's diligent in reminding herself what's important.

Linda makes the daily choice to turn a potentially lousy, curse-these-endless-chores attitude into praise and thanksgiving. And that choice translates into joy for Linda. She chooses joy! Despite the looming drudgery of organizing a squadron of messy little people, she's one of the most joyful gals I know.

In her book *Choose Joy: Because Happiness Isn't Enough*, two-time cancer survivor Kay Warren (wife of author/pastor Rick Warren) observes, "Joy is rooted in gratitude. You cannot have a joyful heart without having a grateful heart. And you cannot be a grateful person and not experience joy."[1]

It's true: gratitude and joy are besties. They hang together. You'll rarely find one without the other. And they adore road trips with their classy chum, awe.

Yes, awe. We get so desensitized by casually bleating the overused flock-o-sheep standard, "awwwe-some," we forget how incredible (and awesome!) that emotion really is. Awe: a simultaneously humbling and electrifying emotion with the power to inspire, heal, transcend our perceived limitations, and rewire our brains.

Awe is the *wow!* factor we feel in the presence of something enormous, astonishing, or supernatural that defies comprehension.

Wow! moments should not be underrated. Scientists are just beginning to recognize the impact of awe on humans. One of the most enlightening investigations is Project Awe, a three-year research project funded by the John Templeton Foundation.

This study found that awe helps people work together

better (realizing we're all a small part of something much larger changes our perspective from "me" to "we"), makes us stop and reflect more, and elicits more humane responses toward others, such as generosity, kindness, and fair treatment. Feelings of awe and wonder also reduce stress and help us to relax; they're actually quite therapeutic and cathartic toward psychological healing and wholeness.

And let's not forget that awe promotes gratitude, which promotes joy!

According to Arizona State University psychologist Michelle Shiota, "For years, awe was thought of as the Gucci of the emotion world—cool if you have it, but a luxury item. But it's now thought to be a basic part of being human that we all need."[2] After reviewing studies by social psychologist Paul Fiff of the University of California at Irvine, writer Paula Spencer Scott concluded, "Awe alters our bodies."[3] How? Awe is a positive emotion that decreases cytokine levels (a marker linked to depression) and increases levels of gratitude and joy.

Unfortunately for crazy-busy moms, stress stifles spontaneous opportunities for experiencing awe-filled transformational moments. To do so, we must purposefully break away from our work, electronic devices, and regular routines (preferably venturing into Papa God's Cathedral of Natural Creation) to expose ourselves to breathtaking landscapes, mighty seashores, magnificent sunrises, powerful waterfalls, the vast star-studded heavens, a baby's perfect tiny toes, and other *wow!* inspiring features of nature our Creator has waiting for us.

But take heart, sister-mom! We *can* take steps—even in

the midst of chaotic, messy mama days—to restock the bare gratitude cupboard. It's actually a BOGO, because where gratitude is, joy will soon follow. Here are some ideas for stocking up on gratitude:

⁂ *Pick a crazy daisy.* Place a bright, cheerful silk daisy (I prefer hot pink) in a pretty vase on your desk or kitchen counter—somewhere visible enough to grab your attention, especially on those crazy days when you feel anything but thankful. Move it around occasionally so you don't get used to seeing it and forget it's there. Let your crazy daisy be a physical reminder to say thank you to Papa God for being present in your life in the midst of craziness. Just a wee nudge to remember He's there, He's aware, and He cares.

⁂ *Schedule weekly Awe Breaks and daily prayer walks.* Add it to your to-do list and then *do it*. Take at least one prayer walk per day for diversity's sake; take the wee ones along in a stroller if need be (the term "wee ones" is soddenly appropriate for diapered babies, don't you think?). A good time for an Awe Break is at night after your little peeps are in bed; step outside beneath a canopy of stars and allow the stillness of the majestic sky to fill you with awe and thankfulness. Intentionally ignite the *wow!* factor in your weary spirit.

Many times, it's the act of being grateful that sparks hope in our bosom (now there's a perfectly good word we don't use often enough) and changes our herspective. We become more focused on our blessings than our stressings. When we look for the Master

Creator in delicate dandelion parachutes, intricate cloud formations, dew-touched spiderwebs, and misty sunbeams reaching down to earth like fingers from heaven, we become acutely aware of His presence, His realness in our everyday. No wonder is too small or insignificant. Oswald Chambers said, "In the ear of God everything He created makes exquisite music."

❋ *Nibble the Bread of Life.* The Bible isn't supposed to be cake for special occasions; it's meant to be bread that we ingest every single day. Chew, swallow, and digest these gratitude-generating verses (look 'em up!). Then you can harmonize with the psalmist, "I will extol the Lord at all times; his praise will always be on my lips" (Psalm 34:1 NIV).

> Colossians 3:15—Let peace rule in your heart (and home) and be thankful.
>
> Colossians 4:2—Devote yourself to prayer and be thankful.
>
> Hebrews 12:28—Be grateful that Christ's kingdom can't be shaken; worship Him with reverence.
>
> Colossians 3:16—Sing with gratitude. (Don't worry, Papa will love it, even if you sound more like a frog than a lark.)
>
> Psalm 100:1—Bring your heavenly Father your gift of laughter (He *loves* to laugh with you; remember, He created your wacky sense of humor!)
>
> Psalm 103:2—Don't forget a single blessing

He's given you (good ideas below on how to accomplish this).

* *Take a gratitude check.* Fix your gaze on something uplifting in the Cathedral of God's Natural Creation (even a picture will do if you can't go outside), and turn off that leaky faucet of worry, complaining, and pickiness that constantly drips into your attitude and eventually drowns awe, wonder, and joy.

  Take a few moments to intentionally enjoy and savor the good things in your past and present. Helen Keller said, "So much has been given to me I have not time to ponder over that which has been denied."

  Life itself is a tremendous gift. We mustn't ever forget that.

* *Treasure the mundane.* Cherish your child's heartfelt hug and how soft and cuddly she is in her jammies; the calming, steamy scent of a cup of hot tea; a surprisingly golden sunset; rich soil in your garden; clean sheets (celebrate NO bedbugs—of course, you appreciate this more if you've ever battled the little devils); the sweetness of a good-night kiss; the hearty laughter of a good friend; a working car; the sun warming your back on a chilly day; children who are able to learn and grow; the privilege of taking care of the ones you love while you still can.

* *Ditch your rude 'tude.* Tough love time. Listen, girlfriend, if you've got a Cheeto on your shoulder (even worse than a chip), get real. From one frazzled mom to another, c'mon, now—don't act like an entitled snob. You may

seriously think you deserve more/need more/are more, but obsessing over it does nothing for nobody. Especially you.

Yearning for more, more, more and ignoring all that your Creator has already done for you doesn't flatter you in the least. You're way above that. Max Lucado calls gratitude being "more aware of what you have than what you don't."[4]

Nothing is more wasteful than sinking precious, limited energy (pining, whining, nagging) into what we wish was different about our lives; it only produces dissent, discontent, and a whopping case of the joy-sucking dully-funks.

Life is too short to make ourselves (and everyone around us) miserable as a wet tabby. In her book, *Only Nuns Change Habits Overnight,* author Karen Scalf Linamen says, "We must work out our gratitude muscle to build it up—exercise it regularly so that it becomes more capable of muscling old grudges and habits out of the way."[5]

✳ *Get daily rest/sleep.* We covered the insomnia assists in chapter 14, but now we're addressing your accompanying sleep-deprived attitude. Not snarky, is it? Get as much sleep as you can, but recognize that during the child-rearing years, you won't get as much as you'd like. None of us do. Period. Don't grouse. Let it go. You can sleep when you're dead. (My granny used to say that, and it always made me laugh.)

For now, make your goal gratitude for the pittance of sleep you do get. Papa will bless you and keep you secure, even on two hours a night. Believe me. I've done it more times than I can count. "Therefore my heart is glad and my tongue rejoices; my body also will rest secure" (Psalm 16:9 NIV).

✳ *Keep track.* A gratitude journal is always a plus. Or a gratitude jar labeled "My Blessings Outweigh My Stressings." Help your kiddos make one too; it's never too early to learn how to be grateful. Write down one blessing every morning on a slip of paper and tuck it in a clear pretzel jar tied with a perky ribbon. By the end of the year you'll have 365 pieces of evidence that Papa God loves you. One glance when you're treading water in the daily stress-pool will remind you that you do have something to be thankful for after all.

Now consider this sobering question, dear friend: What if all you wake up with tomorrow are the things you thanked Papa God for today? Hmm. Certainly throws things into perspective, doesn't it?

In a 1979 column titled "If I Had My Life to Live Over," the late great humorist Erma Bombeck wrote, "Instead of wishing away nine months of pregnancy and complaining about the shadow over my feet, I'd have cherished every minute of it and realized that the wonderment growing inside me was to be my only chance in life to assist God in a miracle."[6]

Let's learn from Erma—the woman who considered "dust" her hobby and admitted she kept her rotten dog only "because he knows too much"—and not waste a smidgen of gratitude to Papa for the gifts we've been given.

Think of stretch marks as pregnancy service stripes.
—JOYCE ARMOR

Navigating the 'Hood

1. On a scale of 1 (low) to 10 (high), where does your gratitude fall on most days? What tends to dictate your gratitude level?

2. What elicits awe in your heart? Name three things that ignite the *wow!* factor in your spirit. How can you use these to raise your gratitude level?

3. Choose two suggestions for stocking your gratitude cupboard and plan to put them into practice this week. Think you can add one more next week?

4. If you wrote an essay called "If I Had My Life to Live Over," what would you change? Would you be able to say that you thanked Papa God enough?

Section 4

· · · · · · · · · · · · · · · · · ·

Mothering Is a Lifetime Gig

*She never quite leaves her children at home,
even when she doesn't take them along.*
—Margaret Culkin Banning

*For the sake of my brethren
[or in our case, sistern]. . . I will
now say, "Peace be within you."*
Psalm 122:8 nkjv

CHAPTER 19

They're Not Crow's-Feet; They're Chuckle Crinkles

Choose Laughter

You know me inside and out, you hold me together.
PSALM 41:12 MSG

~~

Since her two sons became old enough to make face-flushing observations, thirtysomething Heidi made it a point to pull herself together before they saw her in the morning. Nothing fancy, just the bare necessities to start the day—undies, pants, bra, shirt, face splashed, bedhead tamed.

One school morning, Heidi overslept and stumbled out of bed, dazed and bedraggled. When she emerged from the bathroom in the same raw condition in which she'd entered, she was surprised to see her eleven-year-old son sitting on her bed, watching wide-eyed.

"Wow. Now I see why girls need to spend so much time getting ready."

When he realized his mistake (the pillow hurled at his head might have tipped him off), he attempted a desperate save. "But it's okay, Mom—you look, uh, fine. Really. Well, maybe if you just. . .like. . .iron your hair or something. . ."

Motherhood is full of those poop-or-get-off-the-pot moments when we must make the pivotal, attitude-forging decision whether to laugh or cry. Many of our routine, everyday situations are too bizarre, unbelievable, or blatantly disgusting to do anything else.

Sure, sometimes we cry. . .when projectile tears of frustration burst forth before we can stop them. But other times, we do have an option, albeit fleeting. So why not choose laughter? It's contagious. It's healthy. Especially for those young work-in-progress humans at your house learning how to handle stress for the rest of their lives by watching you.

Listen, the odds are *never* in your favor that the day-to-day insanity will cease as long as kids tsunami your home. But you can surf the overpowering wave rather than be scraped along the broken-shell-strewn bottom. Choosing laughter will buoy you to the top.

Face it, mom-friend, hassles and harassment are inherent to the harried 'hood.

A good example is the time I secured my three-day-old newborn in the automatic baby swing so I could make dinner. The swing was in a short, narrow hallway beside the kitchen so I'd have full view of my brand-new bundle of joy while I cooked.

I was sorting through recipes when a strange squish-squashy

sound assaulted my ears. I glanced up and was riveted by the mesmerizing spectacle of green-black baby diarrhea rhythmically slinging from my darling's diaper straight up the wall in front of him—*splat*—and then up the wall behind him with every pendulum swing. *Splat. Splat. Splat. Splat.*

It was a Tough Mudder's nightmare. Only smellier. Speaking of mud (or at least dark, sticky substances), just yesterday my twenty-month-old grandprincess Breeja observed her six-year-old brother squirreling away a chocolate kiss from my candy dish into his front pants pocket. So she proceeded to stuff as many chocolate kisses her chubby little fist could hold into her pocket too.

Only her pocket turned out to be her diaper.

Then she toddled outside on a scorching Florida summer afternoon. Wanna guess the ending? Yep—that's when Breeja learned to amble bowlegged like a cowpoke who'd straddled his faithful steed too long.

Yeppers, these and a million other icky incidents inspired me to compose this little ditty one night while staring at the minefield that was my kitchen floor. Go ahead—sing it aloud to the tune of "Three Blind Mice." Just see if you can stop.

Chunks
by Debora M. Coty, lyricist extraordinaire

Chunks, chunks, chunks;
I'm standing in the chunks.
Chunks, chunks, chunks,
everywhere there's chunks. . .
Bananas and crackers and pizza hunks,

they're gooey and sticky and oh so plump;
Can't tell if they're from Junior's mouth or his rump,
These chunks, chunks, chunks;
Chunks, chunks, chunks.

Well, what can I say? It's not Taylor Swift. . .but give her a few years.

In the spirit of choosing laughter during the nonlethal catastrophes of life, I'd like to close this chapter with ten Coty Near-Facts of Science. Some are from my other books (which you have in your Debora Coty collection, right? *Right?*), but most are brand new and ripe for mom-application. Chuckle heartily!

1. *Summertime Pool Rule*: Taking a kid to a potty break in a wet bathing suit is like peeling the skin off a hot dog then trying to put it back on.

2. *The Bridge Principle*: If you have decent cleavage, wear awesome footwear. People's eyes will then automatically bridge from the top of you to the bottom of you, never pausing to notice the hips in between.

3. *Squirrel Syndrome* (or "How Moms of Little People Talk on the Phone"): Can't finish one sentence before switching to ten more each time you're interrupted. Results in herky-jerky nonsense and cracked nuts deposited all over the place.

4. *Ku-ku-ca-choo Complex*: Grown, mature, *married* women

getting tongue-tied around cute teenage boys. *Yeesh.* It's like you're sucked into a time tunnel and suddenly become the shy, awkward young girl you once were, even though your kids are climbing all over you like rabid monkeys. Guess it's true, we're all still fourteen on the inside.

5. *FAAT—Fabulous Anti-Aging Theory*: FAAT postulates that chocolate actually retards the aging process. What better way to get rid of wrinkles than to fill them out? It's like blowing air into a balloon—all the creases disappear and the surface is smooth as a baby's bottom. Skin works the same way: the fluffier it is, the younger it appears. Plus, the oils in chocolate act as a moisturizer, like the baby's bottom just got lubed with Butt Paste.

6. *Lipstick Morphism*: Activated by the exchange of far-too-scarce funds, newly purchased lipstick magically turns four shades lighter than it was in the store. This brilliant but wicked marketing tool forces you to buy scads more lipstick. Exchanging it would be as classy as returning a toothbrush you used to clean bathroom grout.

7. *Alka-Seltzer Sisters*: The best stress relief women have is each other.

8. *King Conk*: The day after you throw the box away, your appliance will conk out. This is one guarantee you can count on.

9. *Seek and Ye Shall Find Angels*: The special-ops angel search-and-rescue unit tasked with finding missing items and returning them to the exact place you've

already looked six times. Also known as the "If It Was a Snake It Woulda Bit Me Rule." Extra agents are assigned to homes with toddlers.

10. *DRAT—Don't Remember A Thing*: The annoying malady familiar to every mentally overloaded woman. Includes the names of your own offspring.

Beloved inspirational author Liz Curtis Higgs says, "Laughter is how we take a much-needed break from heartache, such that when we turn to face it again, it has by some miracle grown smaller in size and intensity."[1]

My adventurous friend Sonya came to the same conclusion, wryly observing, "Humor is a tool for getting through anything!" while riding a big white mule named Hillary through a coffee plantation in Guatemala.

So here's the formula, sister-mom: Humor + Faith + Perseverance = Survival.

Okay, in a pinch, you *could* survive on just faith and perseverance, but who would want to? Belly laughs are more freeing than burying your Spanx. Life's too short to not snort iced tea through your nose now and then.

• •

Hobbies? I'm a mom. Dismantling gum hairballs is my specialty but I do enjoy an occasional wild excursion to the bathroom alone.
—MEME SMACK

• •

Navigating the 'Hood

1. When was the last time you had to make the pivotal decision of whether to laugh or cry during a nonlethal catastrophe? Which did you choose? Which do you usually default to?

2. Can you remember an incident when enough was too much and you just couldn't hold back the tears? It's okay. Everyone's plumbing springs a leak sometimes.

3. Pause a moment and join me in a rousing round of "Chunks, chunks, chunks. . ." C'mon now, don't be shy—belt it out! It's an earworm; soon you'll be singing it in the shower and pacing yourself with it on your daily mile.

4. Which of the Near-Facts of Science listed in this chapter do you relate to most? They're fun, aren't they? I'm confident that one of these days scientists will prove them to be *real* facts of science. Hey, if you come up with one of your own, I'd love to hear it! Contact me anytime at DeboraCoty.com.

CHAPTER 20

Letting Yourself Go

. . . .

Emotional Damage Control

Let the mighty strength of the Lord make you strong.
EPHESIANS 6:10 CEV

~ ୨୧ ~

When my friend Rebecca's chatty, gregarious, pre-K daughter Gracie thanked the aide helping her out of the car at school one morning, the woman commented, "Your mommy sure knows how to raise polite kids; she should have another baby."

Gracie replied as if this was the silliest thing she'd ever heard, "Mrs. Jones, my mommy can't have any more babies; she had her uterus removed." (Gee, don't all five-year-olds have a working knowledge of the human reproductive system?)

Soon after, Gracie's daddy took her to the father-daughter school dance and was amazed that all the adults knew Gracie by name. Rebecca didn't know why that surprised him; she was sure they also knew the color of his underwear, the amount of time he and Mommy made kissy-face in the morning, and all about her missing uterus too.

Nothing is private when you have kids, is it? TMI should be a middle name.

As our church's Bible Story Lady, I once asked a roomful of preschoolers, "What do you do when someone makes you mad?" A freckled redhead piped up, "Mommy gets mad at Daddy when he toots at the table. She makes him fan his bottom till the smell goes away."

I've had a hard time looking that daddy in the eyes ever after.

Dredging up grace to forgive our kids for their, um, *indiscretions*, can be tough. Not to mention their disobedience, lack of respect, and flat-out defiance. But Romans 13:13 (NLT) sets the goal for our responses: "We should be decent and true in everything we do."

Not easy. Not fun. Not at all how we *feel* at the moment. But our efforts to do so will not go unnoticed.

My friend Judy realized this truth the day she met her husband for lunch at a pizza place. The lady sitting at a nearby table with two young girls got up, walked over, and asked if they recognized her. Judy's jaw dropped. It was the now-grown foster child they'd taken in as a difficult twelve-year-old.

The young woman profusely thanked Judy and her family for the blessing of sacrificial love they'd given her during her short time with them. Now, years later, she was passing it on to her own children.

Sacrificial love. Have you ever thought of your love for your kiddos that way? As a sacrifice? Something that doesn't always come easy; something that costs you—maybe even costs you dearly—yet you're willing to pay the price for the good of your children.

You sacrifice in small ways for your kids all the time—skipping your fave HGTV show to read to your daughter; wearing saggy, ancient underwear so the budget stretches for a new school uniform; posting your grandma's heirloom china on Craigslist so your son can get the tutoring he needs.

Listen, girlfriend, Jesus—who knows a thing or two about love sacrifices—sees all your sacrifices, small and large. He *sees*. He *knows*. And He's incredibly proud of you. You might not think you're much, but He thinks you're to die for.

Yet despite the fact that we're intimately known yet unbelievably still precious to our Savior, we all experience times when we're barely hanging on. Like my cat Sammy-Q.

One morning as I left for work, I punched the garage door remote. As I began driving away, I happened to glance in my rearview mirror and saw something black and white and fluffy dangling from the top of the closed garage door. Strange. It looked like. . . *Uh-oh!* I slammed on the brakes then floored it backward up the driveway.

Sammy-Q had evidently been sitting atop the open garage door—an irresistible ledge for curious felines. When the garage door suddenly began closing, Sammy-Q jogged it like a treadmill but eventually ran out of door. So there he was, helplessly hanging by one claw above a ten-foot drop to the cement driveway.

There are days when we feel like Sammy-Q. And other days when we make our kids feel like Sammy-Q. Oh, not intentionally. Well, most of the time unintentionally [see Deb cringe here]. But when we do unload on them, we can't just ignore that it happened. We need to do emotional damage control.

I'm shaken to my maternal core by this illustration that writer-mom-teacher Tricia Lott Williford calls "Crumpled."[1] It goes something like this:

> Hold a fresh, straight piece of paper in your hands.
> Notice how perfect it is—flat, smooth, undamaged.
>
> Now crumple it up; wad it into a ball. Smash the ball flat. Stomp it with your foot. Tear a piece off.
>
> Okay, now open the paper back up; lay it flat like it was before. Smooth it out—no wrinkles or creases. Replace the torn piece. Exactly like it was before.
>
> Done? No?
>
> Oh, you can't fix it?
>
> Well. . .pick up the paper and apologize. Just tell it you're sorry. Tell it you didn't mean to hurt its feelings or rip it to shreds; it was an accident. Just say you're sorry. Go ahead. That'll make it all right.

Ouch. My heart hurts as the truth in this analogy sinks in. I'll bet yours does too.

I know, sister-mom, I know. You didn't mean it. You didn't mean to wound your child by flinging those jagged words that cut and drew blood. You didn't mean to emotionally crumple him into a ball and stomp on him. Or tear away irreplaceable pieces.

But still, you did. In fit of frustrated passion, you did.

I know, because I did too.

But all is not lost. Papa God isn't finished with our children yet. Or with us.

We can learn from our mistakes and find freedom in redemption. Our future is *not* dictated by our past. We are *not* hopelessly terrible mothers. There's always hope for us if our heart's desire is to become more like Jesus; we just have a bit further to go, that's all. "Therefore if anyone is in Christ, he is a new creation; the old has gone, the new has come!" (2 Corinthians 5:17 NIV).

It's never too late to begin the redemption process. A great way to initiate emotional damage control with your kids is by taking these three steps:

Step 1: Outward. Begin restoring the crumpled relationship with your child by asking his forgiveness. Regardless of his age. Even a toddler needs to see that humility, repentance, and responsibility for one's actions apply to mommies and daddies as well as themselves. Someone wise said, "The formative period for building eternal character is in the nursery." Your children will learn to ask forgiveness—or not—by modeling what you do. Deuteronomy 6 reminds us to model God's values to our kids, "wherever you are, sitting at home or walking in the street. . .from the time you get up in the morning to when you fall into bed at night" (verse 7 MSG).

My daughter, Cricket, who is a much better mother than I ever was, regularly models humility and forgiveness to her children. Because they witness her humbling herself, admitting she lost her temper or made a mistake, and looking them straight in the eyes to ask forgiveness, they pattern their own behavior after hers.

My Mimi heart melted like butter recently when my young grandbuddy, bottom lip trembling, approached me and admitted, "Mimi, I said I obeyed you this morning but I didn't. I'm sorry. Will you forgive me?"

I think I cried more than he did. But we joined hands and asked Papa God to be with us always, celebrated with a forgiveness hug, and proceeded to pelt each other with pillows like it was the most natural thing in the world. And I pray that it will be—that asking forgiveness will come naturally to him for the rest of his life. "Humble yourselves, therefore, under God's mighty hand, that he may lift you up in due time" (1 Peter 5:6 NIV).

Step 2: Upward. Confess your faux pas (oh, let's just call it what it is: sin) and ask Papa God for forgiveness too. Don't worry—He's always standing by with His arms wide open, ready to forgive and forget. "There is therefore now no condemnation to those who are in Christ Jesus" (Romans 8:1 NKJV).

Step 3: Inward. Forgive yourself. Possibly the hardest part of all. To establish parameters on wallowing in the muck of guilt and self-loathing, my advice is to spill to a safe, trusted friend. If we do too much introspection, we sometimes get lost wandering around in there all by ourselves. "Laugh with your happy friends when they're happy; share tears when they're down" (Romans 12:15 MSG). The bigger picture is often clearer when verbalized, and a friend's honesty wrapped in unconditional love helps put our tomfoolery in perspective.

My bosom friend (to borrow Anne of Green Gables' bestie phrase) Jan and I talk each other through self-forgiveness when we lose control or do stupid things that cause ourselves public embarrassment. We inevitably end up laughing more than crying, and it becomes the most cathartic, therapeutic, and healing phone call of the week. (Isn't it mind-boggling how you can follow Christ for decades and still behave like a horse's patootie in certain circumstances?)

Forgiving and asking forgiveness are always going to be part of life; we might as well get used to it now. Then when we're old and gray, our kids won't be surprised when we beg forgiveness for senior moments. Like when my friend Bob's mother gave him a $50 restaurant gift card for his birthday. So generous! After Bob and his wife had enjoyed a lovely meal including hors d'oeuvres and dessert, the server informed him that the card had been previously used and only had $2.76 left on it. *Happy birthday, Bob!*

So from now on, to avoid overreacting then having to apologize for my insane behavior, I've decided to avoid stressful situations like my dog Fenway would; if I can't eat it, bury it, or play with it, I'll just pee on it and walk away.

• •

When you are a mother, you are never really alone
in your thoughts. A mother always has to think
twice, once for herself and once for her child.
—SOPHIA LOREN

• •

Navigating the 'Hood

1. Can you recall a time when you had to deal with the fallout of your kid(s) offering others a little TMI (too much information)?

2. How do you usually deal with forgiveness involving your kids? Are you comfortable asking them for forgiveness when you blow it as a parent? Do they ask for your forgiveness when they mess up? Are you willing to teach them how by your own example? Trust me, it's *never* too late to start!

3. Which step toward emotional damage control is most difficult for you—outward, upward, or inward? What can you do to make it easier?

4. Psalm 103:12 (CEV) is incredibly reassuring: "How far has the LORD taken our sins from us? Farther than the distance from east to west!" Come up with ways you can mirror the forgive-and-forget model Papa God has set for us in the way you interact with your children. (Examples: drop the silent treatment after an altercation; make a plan of action in advance, *before* your next emotional explosion, and then follow through; do something special to show your child she is loved unconditionally following a clash.)

CHAPTER 21

Call Me Thrill Rider

• •

Finding Adventure in the Mundane

Where there is no wood, the fire goes out. . .
PROVERBS 26:20 NKJV

*A*lthough she was my youngest and long weaned, three-year-old Cricket had observed many nursing mothers among our friends. So it seemed quite natural to her to pretend to nurse the Baby Giggles doll she was never without.

Once while we were dining out with our neighbor, an Irish Roman Catholic priest named Father Fitzgerald, Cricket dragged Baby Giggles out of my bag and clutched the doll to her chest in the customary chow-down position.

"Oh, what a lovely baby," Father Fitz crooned. "May I see her face?"

Without missing a beat, Cricket responded, "Not now. I'm milking her."

Later, during a rushed stop at Walmart, I accidentally left Baby Giggles in the car. Within three minutes, Cricket let me (and the whole store) know about my fatal error.

With no time to run back to the car, I soldiered on to the garden department where I added a three-pound bag of bone meal to my buggy. Cricket's wailing turned to cooing as she happily commandeered Baby Bone Meal, who obediently nursed in her arms for the remainder of the excursion. Cricket wouldn't release her death grip even for the cashier to scan the bag.

Back at the car, Cricket refused to swap Baby BM (now wouldn't *that* be a catchy doll name?) for Baby Giggles and profusely showered love on that ridiculous faux infant all day. I had to sneak the silly thing out of her room that night after she fell asleep and spread the bone meal in my rose bed by moonlight so my daughter wouldn't be scarred for life when I disemboweled her little darling.

Now I've never seen a baby quite as—well, I hate to use the word *ugly*—but Baby BM was a sack of fertilizer in every way. Yet Cricket doted on that homely thing as if it were the most beautiful baby in the world.

That was the day I truly grasped the God-given instinctual depth and devotion—and blindness—of a mother's love.

It's a good thing, isn't it? Because our kiddos aren't always terribly lovable.

Especially on those weary, drudgery-pocked days when we're hard-pressed to see anything remotely compelling about our offspring. They rule our roost with an iron fist. Demanding little mess-mongers who cram our days (and sleepless nights) with repetitive chores, endless cleanup, and dull routine.

Ah, routine. . .the stuff that real life's made of while you're waiting for something exciting to happen.

You get up in the morning, throw back a cup of caffeine, and launch into the same routine day after boring day: work, cook, clean up, repeat. Seriously, isn't life made up of 90 percent routine? So easy to overlook as Papa God's intentional blessing.

Yes, I said *blessing.* As in no catastrophe is currently occurring, your health allows you to get up at all, and Papa God has generously allowed you to live to see another sunrise. These are blessings we often overlook.

Gratitude for the mundane keeps our Creator-creation perspective intact. It's the acute awareness that the Source of our often-overlooked everyday blessings—such as a warm breeze, lungs to draw it in, senses to feel its pleasure—is here with us every second, enjoying our enjoyment.

When we look at it this way, the mundane becomes downright thrilling! We see annoyingly noisy kids as happy, carefree children; work duties become a privilege many are without; household chores wouldn't take so long if we lived in a grass hut swarmed by flies.

Routine may be boring at times, sure, but please don't resort to extreme measures to interject excitement like the Vermont mother who thought riding on top of a car with her five-year-old son, hanging on to the cargo rack while traveling fifty miles per hour down the highway, would add a little zip to her day.[1] (She got a year in the slammer for that little thrill ride.)

Or the woman I heard about in India who, after being married fifty-five years, decided she was tired of the same ol' same ol'. So to shake things up a bit, she had in vitro fertilization and gave birth to a baby girl at the age of seventy.[2]

We all like surprises, but not exactly like the one shoppers got in a children's store in a Hong Kong shopping mall when a fifty-five-pound juvenile female wild boar wandered in through a loading entrance, climbed a ladder, and punched a hole through a showroom's ceiling with her sharp hoof. (My guess is she was in search of a good manicure). Crowds squealed as Miss Teenage Piggy, evidently a budding fashionista, jumped to the floor and skittered around the shop, leaving upended mannequins and scattered merchandise in her wake.[3]

Hey, sometimes a girl's just gotta shop, right?

Plenty of excitement in the midst of the mundane was generated (in my gallbladder) when my fluffy white Lhasapoo, Tiffany, decided to buck routine by jumping out the window of a moving car I was driving. I lunged across the seat and grabbed her tail as she disappeared out the window. Tiff dangled there outside the passenger's door until I could pull over and haul her back inside. Gave new meaning to the term "hanging by a thread."

I'll agree, sometimes our mundane lives could use more zing. Maybe we need to shake things up from time to time. But perhaps not car-roof hang gliding, trading in Depends for Pampers, or doggy zip lining. Still, something. . .different. As my granny used to say, "If we always do what we've always done, we'll always get what we've always got."

Here are some ideas for morphing the mundane into everyday adventures:

✳ *Look for the laugh.* It's there, but sometimes you have

to peel away a few layers to see the humor in everyday situations. Like the gal who got up in the wee hours (appropriate phrase, don't you think?) for a potty break without her contacts and reached down to pick up a colorful scarf from the bathroom floor. Suddenly, one end of the scarf rose up and stared at her. Then it flicked its forked tongue. That's because it was a python that had slithered away from her neighbor's apartment and squeezed beneath her door.[4] Didn't even bring over a plate of brownies. *Humph.*

* *Plan getawaycations.* Start saving your pennies for a special trip to a special place. In the meantime, plan monthly, restorative, low-cost mini-vacays for long weekends: borrow camping equipment and explore the great outdoors with friends; visit nearby B&Bs; take road trips to places you've never been. Anticipation is half the fun. Having something exciting to look forward to expands the imagination and quickens the heart like nothing else.

* *Get your bad self down.* Add more music to your life's soundtrack. (No, I didn't say background TV noise—I said *music.* Your brain doesn't process them the same!) Music has the magical ability to speed you up, calm you down, and chase your dully-funks away. Whether you're listening to it or making it (say, how about learning to play a musical instrument, hmm?), music lightens, brightens, and heightens your spirit.

* *Get dirty.* If your face just contorted after reading those two words, get past your dirt-phobic self. It's okay to

get dirty—Yahweh created dirt. He likes the stuff. He designed plants to live there and gave us hands to work the soil while cultivating them. And He created human skin so that grime washes right off. So create a sweet-scented, aesthetically pleasing garden, even if it's a few pots circling a concrete light pole. A living, growing garden will calm you and beautify your living space. And best of all, it'll connect you with the Master Gardener.

It's true, sometimes we forget to be thankful when we get caught up in everyday drama. But, sister-mom, we can't let thankfulness be a casualty of an overstressed schedule. Let's choose to feel blessed, rather than entitled, in our marvelous everyday mundane. Maybe an injection of gratitude is just what the Great Physician ordered.

• •

Relax, sweetie. You will not ruin his
life by making him eat his peas.
—SAGE ADVICE FROM A SWEETLY RIPENED MOTHER

• •

Navigating the 'Hood

1. Fess up now: Are there days you see more beauty in a bag of fertilizer than in your kids? (Don't worry—your secret's safe with me!)

2. Do you ever find yourself drudging through the boring sameness of your life, biding your time until something

exciting happens? Say, what becomes of all those mundane moments/hours/days that you missed actually living in? Are they just tossed away like stale crackers?

3. Relate a time you found unexpected humor in an everyday situation gone awry. Looked for the laugh in any recent catastrophes?

4. Have you stopped lately to thank the Creator of your world for your mundane blessings? You might be surprised how much your her-spective brightens when you become more aware of your everyday, routine gifts!

CHAPTER 22

Morphing This Worrier into a Warrior

Worry

*Let us come boldly to the throne of our gracious
God. There we will receive his mercy, and we will
find grace to help us when we need it most.*
<small>Hebrews 4:16 nlt</small>

⌒~ꝏ~⌒

*I*t was the third sleepless night in a row I'd been worried
sick about my sixteen-year-old daughter. Cricket had just
transitioned from a Christian school to a public high school
and had been the target of two bullies on her basketball team
since day one.

One imposing girl was six feet three inches and the other six
feet one (Cricket was only five three); each outweighed her by
fifty-plus pounds. They resented that new-to-the-team Cricket
was named starting point guard instead of their usual third
Musketeer, so they did everything possible to make Cricket's

life miserable. "Go back to where you came from" became their intimidating mantra. Taunting Cricket at practice and cornering her in the locker room were bad enough; the coach wouldn't intervene, and the other players were afraid to cross the bullies.

When an anonymous death threat arrived in the mail, anxiety began accompanying worry during my midnight mama vigils.

My distraught daughter couldn't eat and cried herself to sleep every night. Each morning she left for school with trembling hands and fearful eyes. I felt like a mirror image; worry was consuming us. It's true: you're only as happy as your unhappiest child.

Hebrews 4:16 (look above) became my go-to for peace and reassurance. My terrified child needed God's mercy and grace more than ever before; therefore, so did I. Every waking hour I boldly approached His throne. And then—

Know what? I'm going to interrupt this story to inject a few words about a mama's major nemesis: worry. Hang tight; I'll finish the story soon.

Another word for *worry* is *wrestle*, agreed? But who are we really wrestling when we worry? The Bible puts it quite succinctly in Ephesians 6:12 (NKJV): "For we do not wrestle against flesh and blood, but against principalities, against powers, against the rulers of the darkness of this age, against spiritual hosts of wickedness in the heavenly places."

Did you catch that, sister worrywart? When we worry, we're wrestling against none other than the devil himself and his band of devious demons. That's Satan: The father of lies. The great deceiver. The ruler of darkness. The power behind all wickedness.

And you know as well as I do that acting alone, we don't stand a snowball's chance in his very, very hot hangout.

Wrestling with the rulers of darkness requires pressure versus pressure; princ(ipalities) versus Prince (of Peace); mano y mano (or in our case, mamasita y demonio). Satan's minions push our kids, and we push back. . .with greater force—with scripture, the omnipotent two-edged sword wielded by the Master of the universe and loaned to mom-warriors when their tribe is threatened.

Put another way, it takes power to bust through a locked door. Or authority, if you have the key to unlock the door. On our own, we have neither. But Papa God has both. When Satan bolts a door to entrap our children, we must turn to the only One who can provide escape. And we do that through prayer. When life knocks you flat on your face, you're in the best position to pray.

I marvel at the miracle of prayer. Isn't it amazing that Papa God hears our prayers on *our* terms? No appointments required. Whenever we want or need to speak to Him. We don't have to set our alarms for 4:36 a.m. to pray because that's the only time He can work us into His schedule. His phone is never turned off.

Yet we tend to think of prayer like a celestial soccer game; if someone plays well with others, follows the rules, and scores enough points, they win. *Ding ding!* God answers yes, the angels sing, everything's peachy.

Nope. The Bible reminds us that Jehovah not only hears the spiritual equivalent of David Beckham, but hears dastardly Debbie too. We can't out-bad His love. The only requirement for a direct hotline to Papa's ear is a contrite heart.

We don't really know how prayer works, but we do know God told us to do it often ("Pray without ceasing," 1 Thessalonians 5:17 NASB), in any crazy place ("From inside the fish Jonah prayed to the LORD his God," Jonah 2:1 NIV), and with our hearts engaged ("Pray that our God will make you fit for what he's called you to be, pray that he'll fill your good ideas and acts of faith with his own energy so that it all amounts to something," 2 Thessalonians 1:11–12 MSG).

Throughout history women have been a dominant prayer force. We learned long ago that prayer is the nerve that moves the muscles in the hand of God.

Did you know that the Gospel of Christ spread across the continent of Europe because of a ladies' prayer group? When Paul and Silas initially arrived at Philippi, they met with a group of women for prayer (Acts 16:13–14), which subsequently begat the first European church and the beginning of the worldwide spread of Christianity. In fact, Lydia, a businesswoman, was the first Christian convert in all of Europe. *Woo-hoo* for girl power!

But despite the proven effectiveness of prayer, we still tend to default to worry. When will we learn that worry is just empty calories? Worry is another kudzu of the spirit, taking over and smothering everything else. It's a sorry waste of energy and a misuse of perfectly good brain cells. (More about worry in my book *Fear, Faith, and a Fistful of Chocolate*).

If we rehearse the worst by worrying, do we really think we'll be better prepared? We won't be. I know it and you know it.

So what's the antidote to worry? "Instead of worrying, pray" (Philippians 4:6 MSG). Yep: prayer. Not just a wimpy little

God-tweet betwixt tub scrubbing and boo-boo bandaging, but the kind of intense prayer that plasters your face on a WANTED poster in hell.

But if you're like most of us, you could use an occasional prayer booster shot to fortify your resilience. So, girlfriend, here are ten simple ways to rejuvenate your prayer life:

1. Before you pray, read the same passage from different Bible translations to broaden your depth of understanding; you'll be surprised how scripture you've read many times will spring to life and speak directly to today's worries.

2. Google then sing (or read aloud) the words to beautiful old hymns of faith such as "Sweet Hour of Prayer," "Just a Closer Walk with Thee," "It Is Well with My Soul," and "Count Your Blessings." And don't forget my personal fave, "How Great Thou Art."

3. Throw a praise fest. Take a nature walk and enjoy the wonders of Papa's creation. Spend your walking time praising the Lord for everything you see and everything He's done for you—butterflies, fat raindrops, relationships, physical blessings, health, happy memories. . .everything. Worship and worry are oil and water; they don't mix. Pick worship.

4. Create your own poem or song about why your faith gives you hope.

5. Pray in a position that's different for you—experience communication with your heavenly Father with a fresh

attitude and posture. Kneel; sit under a backyard tree; raise your hands; elevate your face toward heaven; rip through the woods praising Papa on your ATV (mine's called Sir Lancelot). Be as creative as He is!

6. Write a list of your deepest struggles: problems for which you have no answers, sins that haunt you, people who continually get under your skin. Now take a red marker and write "TRUST" over each one. Lift them up to Him. "The prayer of a person living right with God is something powerful to be reckoned with" (James 5:16 MSG).

7. Get your worship on. Dance before the Lord "with all your might" as David did in 2 Samuel 6:14. Put on your favorite jiving praise music, kick off your shoes, grab the kiddos, and offer back to the Lord all the groovin' moves He's given you.

8. Make a *Marinate List* of ten things you find pure, lovely, admirable, excellent, and praiseworthy (see Philippians 4:8). Make copies for your pocket/purse, car, and work area. These are the things Papa wants you to think about—to marinate in—in order to trump worry with His peace.

9. Convert your car into a rolling cathedral; stock it with your prayer list, praise songs, and inspirational CDs. When another driver cuts you off or you're stuck in a traffic jam, hey, baby girl, do you some church! Replace road rage with prayer and praise.

10. Surprise a friend with a favorite snack, book, or helium

balloon with an uplifting scripture attached. Explain that this is your encouragement gift and now it's their turn to encourage someone else.

Okay, time to finish my opening story. Did prayer suddenly make my daughter's unjust persecution go away? No. But it absolutely helped her persevere with integrity until the end of the school year when both bullies exited stage left. And it made a lasting impression on teammates who watched Cricket lean on supernatural strength not her own. The following season they unanimously voted her team chaplain and co-captain.

Cricket's (and my) desired outcome for that year battling Hades wasn't the same as our Savior's. We wanted short-term behavioral change; His goal was long-term heart change. Sometimes Jesus calms the storm, and sometimes He hands you a paddle.

Remember, in this wrestling match we call life, prayer double-teams all limitations. Worry can't strangle-hold you. The devil can't pin you. With the spiritual equivalent of André the Giant in your corner, *nothing* can hold you back. . . .

✻ There are just nine numbers—look what Bill Gates did with them.

✻ There are eight keys in a musical scale—look what Beethoven did with them.

✻ There are seven colors in the rainbow—look what Michelangelo did with them.

✻ There are six days in a workweek—look what Yahweh created with them.

* There are five fingers on a hand—look what Mother Teresa did with them.

* You are but one little mama—can't wait to see what Papa plans to do with you!

. . . .

*My alarm clock wears footie jammies
and melts my heart every morning.*
—A SLEEPY BUT GRATEFUL MOM

. . . .

Navigating the 'Hood

1. Do you find that worrying often leads to panic, which leads to hopelessness, which makes you feel like you're flunking Faith 101? Please don't fret. As writer Chrystal Evans Hurst, author of *Kingdom Woman,* says, "God is not looking for your perfection; He's looking for your affection."[1] Keep plugging in your spiritual GPS—prayer—dear sister-mom; it'll keep your thoughts and actions from veering off the high road into a ditch.

2. Need a good meme to remind you to pray for your kids? "Pour out your heart like water before the face of the Lord. Lift your hands toward Him for the life of your young children" (Lamentations 2:19 NKJV).

3. Are you more of a petrified worrier than a prayer-fortified warrior? Would you like to change that? Which of the ten prayer boosters will help shoot your mug shot to hell's MOST WANTED list?

4. One of my favorite lines from literature is Atticus Finch's understated advice to his daughter Scout whenever she starts to fret: "It's not time to worry yet" (in Harper Lee's 1960 novel *To Kill a Mockingbird*). I can sometimes hear my heavenly Papa's still, small voice whisper the same to me. Listen closely; I bet you'll hear it too.

CHAPTER 23

Patience Should Be a Verb

. . . .

Perseverance

It's smart to be patient, but it's
stupid to lose your temper.
PROVERBS 14:29 CEV

~ ૭ᶜ ᵔ

*T*he back end of my car dangled over the mountain ledge;
I stared in shock at nothin' but blue sky through my
windshield. What just happened? Why was my car suddenly
pointing heavenward at this gut-churning angle, the front
wheels spinning in midair?

Oh. Yeah. Impatience, that's why. Where there's a will,
there's an idiot. . .

Instead of turning right on the narrow gravel mountain
road—which would've taken me an additional five minutes to
circle around and get where I was going—I tried left-turning
a shortcut off the beaten path. I cut short all right; *too* short.

My back tires started sliding right off the ledge. It felt like a tractor beam was pulling my car backward, even as I pressed harder on the accelerator to urge it forward.

The skidding car suddenly stopped, teetering on its back axle like a crazed seesaw. I realized, with nauseating clarity, that if it slid one more foot, the car would flip and I would be. . .um, not feeling too swell.

Ack! Scarcely breathing, I grabbed my cell phone. No service in the mountains. I laid on my horn. Nobody nearby to hear. So I was on my own. Well, me and Papa God, whom I bombarded with a steady stream of rhino-in-the-road emergency prayer tweets.

Amazingly, the car stayed put. In my mind's eye, I could see the angel back there bracing himself, one hand gripping the mountain and the other my back bumper, keeping me from catapulting over.

But how was I to get out? I couldn't open the driver's door against gravity with the front end of the car elevated like this. I tried; it was like pushing a boulder uphill. If I scooted over to the passenger door, the weight shift might upset the fragile balance of the unstable car and over I'd go.

A still, small voice broke through my panic: "Try your door again. I'll help you."

So in excruciating slow mo, I unbuckled my seat belt, twisted around to place both feet against the door, and shoved with all my might. It felt like a thousand pounds. But it did open the tiniest smidge. After many more tries, I was finally able to shimmy through the narrow opening and drop to the ground.

Be still, my pounding heart. All because I wasn't patient

enough to spare an extra five minutes. *Five minutes.* My impatience almost made me a headline.

Thankfully, impatience doesn't usually incite a life-or-death crisis in our everyday mom-roles. But it does occasionally trigger the urge to kill. You'll likely gnash your teeth in agreement with these triggers a group of young mothers identified as fam-slams that really set them off:

* "I forgot."

* "I dunno."

* NOT listening

* Lack of support from extended family for your parenting style and choices

* Lack of spousal support

* Ingratitude

* Not getting ready on time

* Not pitching in with chores

* Irresponsibility (example: stale, wasted food because the bag wasn't closed)

* Unkindness to pets or sibs

* Not turning off electronic devices

* Endless bickering

* Disrespecting parents

* Attitude of entitlement

* Whining

Bet you could add a few more to your own list, huh? Q: How many mom triggers are exacerbated by impatience? A: All of 'em! As you read the list, you'll know which ones torque your entrails when a sudden spike in blood pressure starts to melt your fillings.

Yet another trigger that tortures moms constantly is waiting. Not being able to have something you want or need *now*. Waiting notoriously unleashes your inner ogre.

Yet mom-life is filled with waiting. . .on dillydallying chirren (as my granny called us kids); distracted spouses; meandering drivers; careless clerks; responses that take for-ev-er; nerve-wracking doctor reports; and oh, so much more.

Even waiting for Yahweh to act.

Like a runt piglet forced to wait for an open spigot, we're stuck "suckin' hind tit" as my ninety-year-old daddy so aptly puts it.

It's no secret that waiting requires patience we often don't have. It feels like perpetual pregnancy—anticipating a baby that's never delivered. We unwittingly adopt the testy disposition of a third-trimester preggers gal. Not pretty. Not nice. But listen to what the Bible has to say about delayed gratification: "Waiting does not diminish us, any more than waiting diminishes a pregnant mother. . . . The longer we wait. . .the more joyful our expectancy" (Romans 8:24–25 MSG).

Joyful? How on earth can we be joyful when we're languishing in wait purgatory? After all, impatience is womankind's archenemy. Like Batman's Riddler or Superman's Lex Luthor, impatience seems to plot our demise, stalk us, then blindside us. That's when the last part of Proverbs 14:29 at the beginning of this chapter kicks in. I call it the Forrest Gump Edict: stupid is as stupid does. (Driving off a cliff is a good example.)

And worst of all, impatience makes us moms lose sight that Papa God's *best* gift is our children. "Don't you see that children are GOD's best gift?" (Psalm 127:3 MSG).

It just doesn't feel like much of a present when squalling kids break out in a wrestling match in the cereal aisle. My friend Calli's solution: "When my kids start bickering, I tell them to stop or I will dance in the middle of the store. I've only had to dance once."

Gift or not, waiting for/on/with kids is an unavoidable part of life, and the Bible says we don't have to be unraveled by it. However can we not? Well, by taking cues from the most patient parent in the world—the heavenly Father who deals with dillydallying chirren every single day (that would be you and me, sister).

Here are three simple and practical ways I've found to draw from Papa God's deep and wide (remember that terrific childhood song?) reservoir of patience when my own pathetic puddle has dried up. I hope they'll work for you too:

1. *Breathe.* Stop and take three deep, cleansing breaths (more if your melting fillings are starting to fuse your teeth together). With each exhale, repeat, "Take it, Lord." Then let Him have it. Resist the impulse to wrestle it back.

2. *Protect precious relationships.* Don't allow your flabbergastation (this really should be a word) to fuel an out-of-control reaction that might cause irreparable damage to relationships you treasure. The most valuable things in your life aren't things; they're people. Cherish them. Despite their snotty noses.

3. *Go ahead, take it hard.* Feel hard, vent hard, then trust hard. If our God is truly sovereign, then everything happens for a reason. We don't like the friction of our jagged edges being sanded down, but we must remember we're each a work in progress. When your youngest tracks doggy doo all over the beige carpet, no use denying your frustration; it's real. It's okay to feel passionately; we're created in the image of a passionate Creator. But don't allow your feelings to take you over. Anger is *not* the boss of you. When things seem to be spiraling south, it helps to use a physical signal to remind yourself Who really is in control (I like a baseball umpire's "safe" sign). Then borrow the chorus to the following little ditty I wrote about who's large and in charge.

Under Control

I woke up at eight; that ole alarm didn't sound.
The kids were late for school and it's the fourth time around.
I'm driving back home and see the homework smiling at me. . .from the seat.
Sometimes motherhood ain't all it's cracked up to be.

I'm standing in the checkout at the grocery store.

The bill's a hundred dollars like it was the week before.

Company's coming; I've got everything here you could eat. . .except meat.

And then my bank card's gone, and all I've got's a dollar on me.

Oooh, help me see. . .

(Chorus) You've got it under control, Lord. You've got it under control.

When it gets out of hand, just help me understand: You've got it under control.

(Bridge) When the day starts to unravel, and Mom starts getting frazzled again,

Help me know that You are there, and I'll stop pulling out my hair

And turn this game over to the One who can win. . .in the end. In the end!

I'm revving the car; I've got a meeting at two.

The engine starts a-smokin' and I don't know what to do.

Just keep it going, keep it rolling to the parking lot at Kmart. It won't start!

And now it's 2:15 and I'm searching for Your joy in my heart.

I rush home from work, got a thousand things to do;

My daughter stands before me with her eyes a-shining blue,

Says, "Mommy, won't you play with me?" and

Throws her little arms around my neck. What the heck?

I guess the dishes can wait and the dog won't

starve before I get back.
Oh, but I know. . .
(Chorus) You've got it under control, Lord. You've got it under control.
When it gets out of hand, just help me understand: You've got it under control.

When impatience threatens to drives us into stupid mode—or off the edge of a mountain—the Lord's patience is our most powerful defense, and He's got plenty stockpiled and ready to share. "We wait in hope for the Lord; he is our help and our shield" (Psalm 33:20 NIV).

Waiting on the Lord to guide us in everyday decisions may at first seem crazy in the pressure cooker of our instant gratification society, but if we do, we'll save ourselves a lot of second-guessing and mind-changing in the end.

Some roads are paved with good intentions; many roads are paved with flat, indecisive squirrels who've second-guessed themselves to death. You and I don't have to be roadkill too, girlfriend.

Papa God offers His shield of protection from impatience, indecision, and irritability. He replaces them with self-control, kindness, and joy. Even when doggy doo smears the sole and frustration smears the soul.

• •

It's not easy being a mother.
If it were easy, fathers would do it.
—FROM THE TV SHOW *THE GOLDEN GIRLS*

• •

Navigating the 'Hood

1. Can you recall a time your impatience got you into trouble?

2. Which are your top three triggers—the fam-slams that most ignite your mom-blaze? How effective are your usual tools to squelch the flames? Do you think it may be time for a new, improved fire extinguisher?

3. When was the last time waiting made you lose your ever lovin' mind? What tends to unleash your inner ogre? Is this the person you really want to be? Is this the person you want your children to be as they emulate their mama?

4. "Feel hard, vent hard, then trust hard": Which of these is easiest for you in the throes of impatience? Which is hardest? What steps can you take to tap into your heavenly Father's stash of patience when yours is "suckin' hind tit"?

CHAPTER 24

Give Yourself Some Grace

Hangin' Tough

He will rejoice over you with great gladness.
With his love, he will calm all your fears.
ZEPHANIAH 3:17 NLT

I asked my daughter and best friend, Cricket Coty Boyer, thirtysomething mother of three and a dedicated, kid-engaging, Christ-focused mom, to share some helpful advice for overrun mothers. Moms who are too stressed to *feel* blessed as they strive to raise godly kids in the everyday trenches.

Cricket's suggestions were so intuitive and, best of all, doable, I thought I'd share them with you verbatim. So as a fitting wrap to this book, here 'tis—encouragement straight from one sister-mom's heart to yours. . . .

First of all, pat yourself on the back and know that you're not alone. When you sit at the park and look around at the other moms, know that every single mother there is probably physically and emotionally exhausted. Most of them are also questioning, "Am I doing enough? Am I good enough?"

Remind yourself that Papa God is *always* enough. If you're living your life for Him as an example to your children, then trust Him to guide your tongue and attitude when you're interacting with them. Even when you falter. Those times are actually excellent growth opportunities for your kids.

I think the best advice I could offer is to be consistent. I've observed an extreme amount of inconsistency in parenting, which produces confusion for the child and creates holes in dependability and structure. The result is wild kids. And frustrated parents.

Consistency, particularly pertaining to discipline, is vital in raising God-honoring children. Telling yourself you're just too tired to deal with little Johnny destroying all your mail or scribbling on your couch with a Sharpie is not okay. This behavior that you're letting him get away with because, "Oh, he's just in his terrible twos. . .or ferocious fives. . .or sassy sevens," is setting him up for more of the same the rest of his life.

Yes, he will continue to make mistakes and test the waters, but it's how you react and discipline *at that very moment* that determines how (and if) he will learn to respect other people and property, feel genuine remorse when he's at fault, and choose to intentionally submit to appropriate authority.

Make no mistake, he's noticing whether there's consistency or not in his weary mother's eyes. I encourage you to woman up, set limits, and stick to them.

Recognize that your consistency is a large contributor to

your child's sense of security. By knowing what consequences to expect, he knows his boundaries and feels safe within their parameters. Whether he pushes against them or not. And he probably will. But a mom's consistent discipline speaks love.

Be diligent in committing yourself to be the example God created you to be. He made you and only you little Emily's mama; no one else in the entire world did He deem right for that role. Just you. Take the privilege and honor of your "Mom" title very seriously.

Be the mom who makes her child feel that *he's* the most important thing in her life, not the electronic device in her hand.

Be the mom who gives herself some grace when she raises her voice at her kids after slaving over a hot, nutritious, homemade meal that they refuse to eat because it has the wrong color noodles.

Then be the mom who exemplifies humbleness by asking forgiveness for the tantrum she threw when the kids refused to eat the noodle dinner.

Turn the electronic babysitter (TV or e-game) off and let your kids go outside and get dirty. Many doctors say this is the healthiest thing you can do to build up your child's immunities. What's more, they'll find playing outside enjoyable and freeing, and it will set a precedent for exploring God's universe and implementing creativity. Really, how often in their lives will they get to squish mud between their toes or cavort in the rain in their underpants? They'll only be children once; they probably won't want to roll around in the dirt as they're leaving for college.

Enjoy nature and teach your kiddos about it: go camping,

take nature walks, build sand castles on the beach. Show your kids the wonder in a mound of hardworking ants and remind them that God made these little creatures too. (Just don't pet them, bud.)

Remember to have patience and an open heart for the thousand times you hear, "Why?" from your little one. Consider this curiosity a good quality; she's learning more about the great big world she lives in. Use those "Why?" moments as an opportunity to establish yourself as the nurturer and teacher of your own child. Learn along with her, rather than becoming exasperated at her incessant questions and sending her to the internet. Google is a tool, not a parent.

Teach your child to have a servant's heart. How else will she learn this other than by helping to make dinner for a sick neighbor or coloring a card for her little friend who is scared about moving? Find ways to show your child how to be compassionate— an ambassador of her heavenly Father—by reaching out in small acts of kindness as Papa's love with skin on it.

Teach your children the power of prayer. Make a point to hold hands with them and pour out your own prayer requests. Oh, spare them details of the mature struggles and emotions you're dealing with, but let them know you're not perfect and that you need God's help in handling daily situations too.

Make sure your world stops every single night to have that precious prayer time with them. It's a good time to talk about forgiveness and list the things you're thankful for that Papa God has provided. Keep a prayer box (a decorated shoebox with a slit in the lid) for your child to drop in a prayer request anytime, day or night. Review the prayer requests together once monthly; this is a great way for a child to see objectively how God answers prayer with a yes, no, or wait awhile.

Do daily devotions with your children over breakfast. There are countless kid-friendly devotions out there that are short, sweet, and to the point. What better way to start the day and teach them that God's Word has real value and application to our lives?

Show your kids that your husband is important to all of you by making a big deal when he walks through the door. Even if you're feeling frazzled, drop everything and greet him with a big embrace. You're embedding in your kids a biblical model for their own future marital relationship, plus you're giving your husband the affection he craves and the respect he needs from you. Everybody wins.

Make date night a priority. Not only is it healthy to have that one-on-one time with your spouse, but it's also important to show your kids your priorities and how much you love Daddy. Research suggests one couple-only date per week, but in most young moms' busy lives, once per month is a miracle and more realistic.

How to pull it off? Ask a relative to babysit (no, you can't have my mom—Debora is permanently reserved!), or do a date swap with another couple you trust. Or ask your church youth director about a reliable teen babysitter. Before your date is complete, pin down your next date night so you don't let it slip away. Be religious about this: do it for your mental and marital health. You'll find yourself experiencing much-needed joy with your husband and the intimate laughter you shared while dating.

Your kids can sense tension between the two of you, but

when you're cooperating as one, the house will transform into a peaceful haven instead of being a minefield of fragile eggshells.

Many of my friends complain that their spouses don't help them enough. Date night is a great time to sensitively (as in don't dump on him all at once) pour your heart out and explore areas where you can be of service to each other and feel that your love language is being acknowledged. (Dr. Gary Chapman's book, *The Five Love Languages,* is a must-read for all couples.)

Your husband won't know—unless you plainly tell him—that you've bottled up steam over that forgotten garbage for two long weeks. Or that you're in dire need of help with the 3:00 a.m. bottle feeding so you can get a few consecutive hours of sleep. Or anything else that's keeping your panties in a wad.

You may be surprised how much your husband has *not* picked up on when you thought your signals were loud and clear.

Also use this time (date night) to tell your husband you appreciate how hard he works at his job and at maintaining the yard (or whatever regular chores he does) and how much it meant to you when he stepped in to help with that pile of laundry. Men thrive on words of affirmation, and they most definitely need to feel appreciated in order to step up even higher.

Yes, I know. It's a lot. A *lot.* If you feel like you're the full-time manager of an important institution, you're totally right—you are. That's what our Creator created moms to do: manage. You, my friend, are a domestic manager. See for yourself in Proverbs 31:10–31: the "ideal" woman is praised as a savvy manager of her family, home, and business.

Papa God always knew we could handle the pressure.

Sure, motherhood is a pressure cooker. But like my dear ole mama says, pressure creates both diamonds and volcanoes. Do we want to sparkle or spew? It's our choice.

• •

Just look at all these moms making stuff they found on Pinterest and I'm over here just trying to take a shower.
—MEME SMACK

• •

Navigating the 'Hood

1. Is implementing consistent discipline difficult for you on a daily basis? Why? Is this something you'd like to work on? If so, take a few moments now to brainstorm ways to improve.

2. Do you ever feel like a lone mama-wolf? Like—whether you're married or not—you're raising your wild, hungry pack all by yourself? We all feel that way at times. . .but it doesn't have to be a permanent feeling. How can you better engage your spouse by sharing responsibility?

3. Have you considered a date night at least once a month? Perhaps you should, my friend. I like to think a contributing factor to Cricket's strong support of them was witnessing her father and I faithfully take date nights while she was growing up. They truly make a difference in a woman's quality of life (not to mention her sanity) by keeping spousal communication lines open, hearts connected, and family goals mutual.

4. In your role as domestic manager of your home, how can you cultivate a spirit of cooperation among your family members?

CHAPTER 25

So How Does This Mom-Gig End?

. . . .

Living in Hope

Christ gives me the strength to face anything.
PHILIPPIANS 4:13 CEV

～～ఎ～

*J*t was a bittersweet testimony to the depth of a mother's love when actress Debbie Reynolds unexpectedly passed away one day after her beloved daughter, Carrie Fisher (of Star Wars fame). Although moms everywhere nodded solemnly in poignant understanding, it seemed shocking to the rest of the world that broken heart syndrome is a real thing.

Is it so hard to believe that a mother's devastated heart can actually cease beating because of a surge of stress hormones brought on by overwhelming grief?

Not for moms. Because we know the bond between a mother and her child is stronger than life itself.

On a less lethal level, moms experience heartbreak all the time.

Whether the heartbreak is due to infertility, miscarriage, dashed expectations, imploded dreams, or disappointment in the decisions our children make, you and I both know how it feels to have a shattered heart that inexplicably keeps on beating. Its hollow, jeering percussions keep us physically alive while haunting our almost-dead spirits.

Broken-heart stories are all different, but the result is the same: damaged hope. At the time, we simply cannot believe things will ever get better.

During my worst period of mom-heartbreak, hope gradually diminished as I sank into a deep depression following six heart-wrenching miscarriages. My raw wounds were so sensitive and easily scalded that I distanced myself from the Lord and my faith for two long desert-dry years. I felt completely alone and utterly lost.

At my lowest point, Papa tenderly reached down to me with His customized mercy and began chipping away at the rock that had become my heart, until it was finally disintegrated and replaced with a warm, feeling, *living* heart. "I will give you a new heart and put a new spirit in you; I will remove from you your heart of stone and give you a heart of flesh" (Ezekiel 36:26 NIV).

Many women struggle with depression at some point in their lives: postpartum (following childbirth), kids-partum (empty nest), brain-partum (menopause), or anytime in between. If you're one of us, or know someone who is, you can find more about dealing with depression in my book *Too Loved to be Lost,* and further details about my personal restoration in the "Lost and Found" chapter of the original

Too Blessed to Be Stressed (the "mama book" from which offspring like the book you're reading right now were birthed).

You met my daughter, Cricket, in the last chapter. With her permission, I'd like to share her incredible mom-story with you because it's all about hope, the topic of this final chapter. To truly grasp the wonder of her story, you need to understand that for her entire life, all Cricket ever wanted to do was be a mother (remember Bone Meal Baby?). She was positive it was her destiny. When she married Josh, even their wedding vows overflowed with hopes and dreams for a large family.

But the shocking reality of infertility soon set in. After years of traumatizing tests, fertility treatments, and uncomfortable surgeries, Papa God blessed Cricket and Josh with a healthy son, Blaine, and they were happy, so happy. That was miracle number one.

More tests, expensive treatments, and another painful surgery. But no baby. Four different fertility specialists informed her all possibilities had been exhausted and there would be no further biological babies in their future. Despite heartache and disappointment, Cricket's hope stayed alive. She kept praying for divine intervention.

Cricket and Josh began foster-to-adopt proceedings, filling out reams of paperwork and undergoing numerous classes and home inspections. The day finally arrived for the last home inspection before all requirements were completed. But that inspection was never to be; Cricket had to cancel the appointment because she was sick.

She was sick because. . .she was *pregnant*! Miracle number two.

But her excitement was soon submerged by the misery that hyperemesis gravidarum (HG) brings. Relentless nausea and uncontrollable vomiting led to a complete shutdown of her digestive system. By her fourth month, Cricket was bedbound with IVs, unable to keep anything down and weak as a kitten. She couldn't perform even the most basic self-care tasks.

After dozens of blown IVs due to collapsed, dehydrated veins, a PICC line and abdominal pump were inserted to supply liquid nourishment, bypassing her stomach. It seemed to be working at first, but during her fifth month, Cricket was rushed to ICU with a blood clot, fever, and convulsions due to a dangerous virulent infection. The constant pain was nearly unbearable. Her confused body went into labor in an attempt to rid itself of the infection.

To save Cricket's life, doctors were forced to give her medications they usually don't give pregnant women. No one knew what effect they might have on the baby. . .if the baby even made it to term.

Hope waned to a sliver. I was on my knees praying so much, I declare I wore out two rugs.

But wait. . .Papa God was up to something.

In the middle of this massive mess, out of the blue one day a young single gal—friend of a friend—approached Josh at work. She was pregnant and had been praying long and hard about what to do; she felt that God had pointed out Cricket and Josh as the very ones to provide a loving, stable, Christian upbringing for her baby. Would they consider it?

Are you kidding me? Would they ever! Having not just one baby but *two*? Unfathomable joy! It was just the infusion of hope Cricket needed to tough out those last few months.

The brave birth mother invited Cricket to participate in the baby's delivery and cut the umbilical cord. No amount of illness could keep Cricket from being there to cuddle that sweet baby girl in her arms. Thirteen days later, Cricket gave birth to an amazingly healthy baby boy.

We call them twins from different mothers. Miracle number three.

You know, Papa God doesn't always send miracles in clumps like He did for Cricket. But. . .sometimes He does.

Papa God doesn't always take two years to haul us out of our pit of despair like He did for me. But. . .sometimes He does.

And therein is hope. We never know what He's gonna do.

"You were tired out by the length of your road, yet you did not say, 'It is hopeless.' You found renewed strength, therefore you did not faint" (Isaiah 57:10 NASB). If your hope tank is sucking air, tape this hope-restoring verse to your bathroom mirror and read it aloud every morning.

We all need hope, dearest sister.

Hope that whatever hardship motherhood throws at us, things will get better. Even in the worst-case scenario—from a mother's perspective—if your child has been called home, you have the hope of seeing them again in heaven. That's why it's imperative that we share the hope of salvation with our children so that we'll be together with Jesus for eternity.

Listen, it ain't over yet. We may not always be able to see His hand working behind the scenes, but a solid, indisputable truth we can count on is that our God is *always* up to something.

Even when the outrageous behavior of our offspring

flattens us with shock waves; even when we find evidence of unacceptable choices in our teens' bedrooms; even when we wear knee holes in six rugs praying for our prodigals. There's still hope. " 'There is hope for your future,' says the LORD. 'Your children will come again to their own land' " (Jeremiah 31:17 NLT). (You can find more about praying specifically for prodigals in *Too Loved to be Lost*.)

As jarring as it is to admit, mothers *never* stop being mothers. We'll always care about, fret over, and fiercely love our kids—bone of our bone and flesh of our flesh. Our Creator hardwired us that way; we relentlessly love our children like He relentlessly loves His (that would be you and me!).

Sometimes we try to tone down that ferocious mama-bear protective instinct, but it rarely disappears entirely. Trust me on this—my ninety-year-old mother still wants to know what I ate for breakfast (hey, I wear big-girl panties now; I draw the line when she asks for an itemized list of my daily fiber intake).

Despite the heartbreak we've endured—no, *because* of it—moms need hope.

Hope isn't just an emotion; it's a perspective, a discipline, a way of life. Hope is a journey of choice. For believers, hope is vital to a dynamic, thriving faith. . .one of the big three that will remain to the end of time: faith, hope, and love (1 Corinthians 13:13).

Hope is a glimmer in the darkness; the buttercup lifting its delicate head from a charred field; that supernatural strength to persevere when all seems lost. Hope, dear sister, is simply Jesus. I pray that you've found Him in these pages.

For Jesus is the ultimate source of hope. We can live

without many things, but we cannot live without hope. It's the air we breathe, the water that invigorates every molecule of our being, the motivation that drives us. Hope enriches and empowers us, connecting us with our Papa God.

Hope is the essence of our faith. It's the foundation and the finale. And it's the most priceless heirloom we could ever pass on to our children.

• •

I remember my mother's prayers and they have always followed me. They have clung to me all my life.
—Abraham Lincoln

• •

Navigating the 'Hood

1. Do you have a broken-heart experience in your life? Does it still hurt to talk about it? Have you consulted the Great Physician about broken-heart surgery?

2. How would you currently rate yourself on a 1 (low) to 10 (high) hope scale? Have you ever dropped below 3? When and why?

3. How do the promises in Isaiah 57:10 and Jeremiah 31:17 relate to your own mom-gig? Do they awaken in you a glimmer of hope?

4. Remember, it ain't over yet; Papa God is *always* up to something. How do these hope-filled truths apply to you and your family?

Notes

Chapter 1: PMS: Pretending Mom's Sane

1. Brunton, P.J. & Russell, J.A. *"The Expectant Brain: Adapting for Motherhood." Nat. Rev. Neuroscience.* 9, 11–25 (2008).

Chapter 3: Unbuttoning My Attitude

1. Skinner, Victor. "Elementary School Mother Chokes, Threatens to Kill Daughter's 'Bully.'" eagnews.org, December 17, 2014. (accessed February 28, 2018).

Chapter 5: Prison Break

1. Prooday, Victoria. "Why Are Our Children So Bored at School, Cannot Wait, Get Easily Frustrated and Have No Real Friends?" https://yourot.com/parenting-club/2016/5/16/why-our-children-are-so-bored-at-school-cant-wait-and-get-so-easily-frustrated. (accessed February 28, 2018).

Chapter 6: I'll Pencil You In at 4:53

1. Frejd, Sylvia Hart. "Peace in a Digital World." *Just Between Us.* 44–45 (Fall 2017).
2. McGregor, Jerry. *40 Ways to Get Closer to God,* (Ada, MI: Baker Publishing Group, 2011).

Chapter 8: Thinking Outside the (Sand)Box

1. Sandifer, Sarah. "Don't Worry, It Gets Better." http://www.gatherandgrow.co/dont-worry-gets-better/ (accessed February 28, 2018).

Chapter 9: Becoming You-Nique
1. "No, Your Kids Aren't Killing You," *Tampa Bay Times*, March 19, 2017.

Chapter 11: Too Blessed to be Obsessed
1. Hoagland, Elizabeth. "Happy Holy Week!" https:// elizabethhoagland.com/category/family/page/7/ (accessed February 28, 2018).

Chapter 12: Chocolate Caulks Relationship Cracks
1. Karen Scalf Linamen quote. *Pillow Talk* (Ada, MI: Fleming H. Revell, 2004).

Chapter 13: Detoxifying My Stinky Face
1. Kanallakan, Amber. "Focused Motherhood: How To Look Beyond the Mess." Channelmom.com, Mar 9, 2017 (accessed February 28, 2018).

Chapter 14: Zombie in Sweats
1. Oz, Dr. Mehmut, "A New Bedtime Story." parade.com, January 22, 2012
2. This list includes excerpts from my book *Mom Needs Chocolate: Hugs, Humor and Hope for Surviving Motherhood* (Ventura, CA: Regal), 2009. Now available through Baker/Revell.
3. 2017 Nielsen report.

Chapter 15: Mommas in the Trenches
1. Tomlinson, Shellie Rushing. "Lessons from a Fighting Rooster." www.belleofallthingssouthern.com, May 23, 2015 (accessed February 28, 2018).

Chapter 16: My Hairstylist Is from Oz

1. Peter T. McIntyre, "Peter T. McIntyre Quotes," GoodReads, https://www.goodreads.com/quotes/7969079-confidence-comes-not-from-always-being-right-but-from-not.

2. Ruth Bell Graham, "Inspiring Words from Ruth Bell Graham," The Billy Graham Library, December 23, 2011, https://billygrahamlibrary.org/inspiring-words-from-ruth-bell-graham/.

Chapter 17: Ripening Isn't Just for Bananas

1. Original story found in Constance B. Fink, "Faithful God," *Just Between Us*, Fall 2014. Kellie Knapp, now a mother of three, blogs at claypots.org.

Chapter 18: Gratitude Is Glade for the Soul

1. Warren, Kay. *Choose Joy: Because Happiness Isn't Enough* (Ada, MI: Revell, 2013).

2. Paula Spencer Scott, "Feeling Awe May Be the Secret to Health and Happiness," *Parade* Magazine, October 7, 2016, https://parade.com/513786/paulaspencer/feeling-awe-may-be-the-secret-to-health-and-happiness/.

3. Ibid.

4. Max Lucado, "Authors: Max Lucado," AZ Quotes, July 4, 2017, http://www.azquotes.come/quote/863165.

5. Linamen, Karen Scalf. *Only Nuns Change Habits Overnight* (Colorado Springs, CO: Waterbrook Publishing, 2008).

6. Bombeck. Erma. "If I Had My Life to Live Over," https://mygratitudelife.wordpress.com/2011/08/10/day-179-if-i-had-my-life-to-live-over/ (accessed February 28, 2018).

Chapter 19: They're Not Crow's Feet; They're Chuckle Crinkles
1. Liz Curtis Higgs, *Joy for the Journey: Morning and Evening Devotions* (Nashville, Tennessee: Thomas Nelson, 2014).

Chapter 20: Letting Yourself Go
1. Tricia Lott Williford, "Crumpled," blog post, February 10, 2017, www.tricialottwilliford.com.

Chapter 21: Call Me Thrill Rider
1. "Mother Admits Riding Atop Vehicle With Son," *Tampa Bay Times*, June 20, 2015.
2. Savannah Fish, Marcus Leshock, "70-Year-Old Indian Woman Gives Birth to First Child," Chicago WGN9, May 12, 2016.
3. "Boar Pays Hong Kong Mall a Visit," *Tampa Bay Times*, May 12, 2015
4. "Woman Finds Python during Nighttime Potty Visit," *Tampa Bay Times*, January 18, 2015.

Chapter 22: Morphing This Worrier into a Warrior
1. Hurst, Chrystal Evans. *Kingdom Woman* (Colorado Springs, CO: Focus on the Family Publishing, 2013).

Acknowledgments

I'd like to heap great green gobs of gratitude upon the wonderful people whose invaluable input keeps my *Too Blessed to be Stressed* dream alive and kicking:

* Greg Johnson: my fabulous agent at WordServe Literary.

* Kelly McIntosh: if ever there was an editor who could double as a bestie, it's you!

* My awesome team at Barbour Publishing—from book conception to graphics to layout to distribution, you all do a fantastic job. My never-ending thanks!

* Chuck Coty: my love, my leader, and my laughing partner, forty years and counting.

* The beautiful people who make me a blessed mama: Matthew (and Rebecca), Cricket (and Josh), and grands, in order of birth: Blaine, Breeja, Breydon, and Mason.

* All my BFFs (Blessed Friends Forever) who've graciously shared chuckles, wisdom, and heartwarming mom-stories with me: Carly Johnson, Debbie Cali, Cricket Coty Boyer, Evelyn and Ralph Mann, Charmaine Andrews, Morgynne Northe MacDougall, Jan and Jeremy McRae, Kim and Lyann Rate, Judy Roney, Sonya Biggs Gissy, Gracie and Rebecca McRae Steele, Sandi and Bob Dorey.

* Awesome Facebook pregnancy story contributors: Kitty, Sam, Veta, Kristi, Pamela, Betty, Judy, Sue, Season, Kat,

Yvonne, Karen, Kim, Wendy, Jen, Elizabeth, Leondra, Karen, Cheryl, Calli, and Ella.

* Terrific professionals and writers whose quotes and contributions add so much to this book: Sarah Sandifer; ChannelMom.com blogger Amber Kanallakan; Dr. Mehmet Oz; Shellie Rushing Tomlinson; Victoria Prooday, OTR; Elizabeth Hoagland; Heidi Chiavaroli; Paula Spencer Scott; Tricia Lott Williford; Carlo D'Este; Janette Barber; and Kelli Knapp.

* Above all, credit and praise go to my beloved Papa God, who constantly amazes me with His easy ability to flip a too-stressed day into a too-blessed day.

Meet the Author

Debora M. Coty is a popular speaker, columnist, Bible student, and award-winning author of numerous inspirational books, including her bestselling Too Blessed to be Stressed series.

Debbie loves swatting a little ball around a tennis court, experimenting with recipes, raising ruckus with girlfriends, playing with her grandbuddies, and hiking Smoky Mountain trails with her desperately wicked pooch, Fenway.

Visit Debora at www.DeboraCoty.com to say hi or share a funny story, book Deb for a speaking event, sign up for her free e-newsletter, catch the latest craziness by subscribing to her *Too Blessed to be Stressed* blog, or join Deb's BFF (Blessed Friends Forever) Club, a community of fun-loving gals who adore chocolate, laughing, and Jesus!

And while you're at her newly renovated website, be sure to check out all of Debora's Too Blessed to be Stressed books:

Too Blessed to be Stressed (the original "mama" book that gave birth to the other "babies"; also available in Spanish)

Too Blessed to be Stressed Cookbook
(over 100 stress-free recipes, each requiring less than 20 minutes' hands-on prep)

Too Blessed to be Stressed Coloring Book (helps you decom-stress by coloring your way to calm)

Too Blessed to be Stressed: 3-Minute Devotions for Women (over 200,000 copies sold!)

Too Blessed to be Stressed Planner (lovely and popular purse-sized planner, updated yearly)

Too Blessed to be Stressed: Inspiration for Every Day (beautiful 365-day devotional)

My Prayer Journal: Too Blessed to be Stressed (creatively brings more depth to your prayer time)

Too Blessed to be Stressed Perpetual Calendar (a quickie inspirational chuckle for each day)